# NATIONAL INCOME AND SOCIAL ACCOUNTING

Harold C. Edey
*Professor of Accounting at the London School of Economics*

Alan T. Peacock
*Professor of Economics in the University of York*

Ronald A. Cooper
*Reader in Economic and Social Statistics in the University of York*



HUTCHINSON UNIVERSITY LIBRARY
LONDON

HUTCHINSON & CO (*Publishers*) LTD
*178–202 Great Portland Street, London W1*

London Melbourne Sydney
Auckland Bombay Toronto
Johannesburg New York

★

*First published 1954*
*Second (revised) edition 1959*
*Reprinted 1961, 1963, 1965, 1966, 1967*
*Third (revised) edition 1967*
*Reprinted 1969*



*Printed in Great Britain by litho on smooth wove paper by Anchor Press, and bound by Wm. Brendon, both of Tiptree, Essex*

09 036763 4 (cased)
09 036764 2 (paper)

CONTENTS

## PART III

## FURTHER ANALYSIS

# PREFACE TO THE THIRD EDITION

Since the last edition of this work considerable changes have taken place both in the scope and content of official economic statistics of national income and expenditure and in their use for both short-term and long-term economic planning. In particular, major improvements have been made in the calculation of the expenditure side of national income and in financial statistics, a new input-output table has been prepared and official use of national income accounting methods have been fully deployed in the long succession of documents produced by the Treasury, National Economic Development Office and the Department of Economic Affairs. These developments, as well as the growth of empirical research in universities and research organisations, have transformed national income and social accounting from a relatively specialised part of economic statistics into an essential element in the training of economists and economic statisticians.

This edition represents, therefore, a completely revised version of the earlier ones. The first three chapters appear to have stood the test of time and contain only minor modifications. Chapter 4 now includes a simple illustration of the firms' operating and appropriation accounts which offers a more convenient link with Part III of the work. Chapter 5 has been completely revised and more up-to-date data are used to complete the national accounts. Chapter 6 has been slightly simplified and account taken of recent changes in official measures of real product. Chapter 7 and Chapter 8 contain major changes which are designed to offer the reader guidance on the logic of the use of national accounts for economic policy purposes. The tables in Chapter 9 have needed slight re-arrangement. It has been possible in Chapter 10 to offer practical illustration of the flow of funds in the United Kingdom using data to be found in *Financial Statistics.* Finally, the bibliography has been brought up-to-date.

The original authors are very grateful to Mr R. A. Cooper, Reader in Economic and Social Statistics, University of York, for agreeing to collaborate in this revised version. He has brought to the book his extensive knowledge of official practice emanating from his previous career as a statistician with H.M. Colonial Office and H.M. Treasury.

Friends and colleagues, too numerous to mention, have been kind enough to offer comments and criticisms which have also influenced this revision.

*May 1967*

# Part I
# The framework of social accounting

# I

# THE NATURE OF NATIONAL INCOME AND SOCIAL ACCOUNTING

## 1. *Introduction*

Before an economist can make useful general statements about economic activity, he must have some suitable description or picture of this activity. This is so whether he is called upon to advise politicians; to advise business men about the effect on one or more sections of the economy of possible changes in other sections; or to perform the not unimportant task of helping students and others to understand more about the nature of the complex economic relationships which govern our lives in the present-day world.

Description can take the form, on the one hand, of minute examination of individual parts of a system or, on the other, of studies of a more abstract character. Much of economics is, indeed, concerned with the description of the growth and form of particular social institutions. However, for the purpose of understanding the network of relationships which make up the economy as a whole, a more abstract approach is required. In applied economics this study is associated, among other things, with the study of national income or social accounting. (In this book, except where the context requires otherwise, we shall assume that 'social accounting' embraces 'national income accounting'.) Social accounting, then, is concerned with the statistical classification of the activities of human beings and human institutions in ways which help to us understand the operation of the economy as a whole.

The field of studies summed up by the words 'social accounting' embraces, however, not only the *classification* of economic activity, but also the *application* of the information thus assembled to the investigation of the operation of the economic system. Accordingly, in this volume we shall be concerned with the analytical as well as the statistical elements of the study, and thus with the connexions between (*a*) social accounting statistics in the narrow sense; (*b*) theoretical 'models' of the economic system which are intended to help us visualise the working of the system and as an aid to the informed guesses about the economic future which we like to call 'predictions'; and (*c*) the real world. We can, in fact, regard the preparation of social accounts, for some purposes at least, as an attempt to assign magnitudes to some of the symbols of theoretical models, just as a natural scientist attempts to fit numerical values, determined by his observations of phenomena, to symbols in the theoretical mathematical expressions which (approximately) describe these phenomena, though the nature of the data imposes on the economist a very much rougher approximation and much cruder 'models' than would satisfy most natural scientists.

### 2. *A general description of economic activity*

One general description of the economic activity of a given region is provided by a numerical statement of the results of that activity in the form of a statistical estimation of the value of total 'production' of goods and services over a particular period of time and of its allocation as between 'consumption' on the one hand and 'adding to wealth' or 'investment' on the other. (The significance of 'value' in this context will be discussed later. For the time being, the reader should assume that 'value' means 'market value'.)

By 'production' we mean the organisation of human activity with the object of bringing into existence, at given places and times, valuable goods and services. 'Production' in this sense does not necessarily imply the *making* of the commodity: it is 'production' to move a commodity already in existence—perhaps a natural gift of nature—to another place, or to hold it through time if, thereby, *value* is added.

By 'consumption' we mean the enjoyment, usually accompanied by some measure of physical destruction, of the fruits of production in a way that satisfies the wants of members of the community. (It is necessary, however, to point out here that, as a matter of statistical convenience, it is usual to assume that commodities have been 'consumed' as soon as they pass into the hands of the 'consumer'—the person whose wants, or whose dependents' wants, they will satisfy—even though the physical process of consumption may last days, weeks or even years.)[1] Consumption may take the form of

[1] Houses are an exception, as we shall see.

enjoyment of commodities by the members of individual households or of public consumption in which certain needs, such as those for education, street cleaning, or defence, are paid for collectively through the medium of the State rather than by direct purchases by individuals in their personal capacity.

'Adding to wealth' or 'investment' or 'capital formation' arises to the extent that commodities produced in a given period are not consumed in that period, thus remaining available for future consumption, or for use in the production of other goods and services for future consumption. It is to be noted that when we speak of 'investment' we must be clear whether we are thinking of a 'net' or a 'gross' addition to the national wealth. In the course of a given period, some of the economic resources in existence at the beginning of the period will be used up through a running down of the stocks of raw materials or finished or partly finished goods available at the beginning of the period; and by the physical deterioration of the type of goods used for production that we call 'capital equipment' or 'fixed capital', such as plant and machinery; and both kinds of resources may lose value through 'obsolescence'—that is, changes in tastes of final consumers, or improvements in methods of production of competitors.

There is a certain ambiguity in the terms 'gross investment' and 'net investment'. When used in a technical sense—as it will be in the rest of this book—'gross investment' refers to the *gross* investment in fixed capital, as defined above, plus, or minus, as the case may be, the *net* change in stocks of all kinds. (This convention is probably due to the statistical difficulty of ascertaining the *gross* addition to stocks in a given period.) If, however, a deduction is made for 'wear and tear' and obsolescence of capital equipment—that is, of 'fixed capital'—the resulting figure is called 'net investment'. Such a deduction is commonly called 'depreciation'.

If we neglect transactions with foreigners, we can summarise the economic activity of a region by using the following simple identities (an identity is an equation which must always be true, whatever values are given to the individual symbols) where all the quantities relate to *values*:

*Production*, or, in technical language, *gross national product*= *consumption* plus *gross investment*=*consumption* plus *net investment* plus *depreciation*.

This can also be written:

*Gross national product* minus *depreciation=net national product= national income=consumption* plus *net investment.*

One of the main statistical problems arising from any attempt to assign numerical magnitudes in this kind of description of economic activity is associated with the attempt to reduce all the various components of the gross national product, consisting of a multifarious variety of goods and services from bus rides to seismographs, to value terms. However, the fact that, in developed economies at least, commodities are, in general, not consumed or disposed of by the persons who individually produce them, but are exchanged for a common medium, money, simplifies the problem to some extent, for there are a multitude of records of such exchanges expressed in value terms.

The idea of a general description of economic activity in terms of a record of national production or output, and its disposal, is part of the classical tradition in economics whereby 'economic welfare' is related to changes in the 'real' output of goods and services, that is to the value of the output, adjusted for changes in the general price level. Thus the first quarter of this century saw, on the one hand, the famous studies of national income statistics by Sir Arthur Bowley and the late Lord Stamp and, on the other hand, the attempts of Professor A. C. Pigou to formulate the concepts of economic welfare more precisely than had formerly been the case. From these pioneer studies, many interesting developments have taken place, such as attempts to make international comparisons of output and productivity, standards of living, distribution of incomes, and so on. The emphasis in this kind of study is on the historical development of the economy and thus on changes over time in such important variables as the production per head of the community, the distribution of incomes, the level of gross and net investment, and so on. This part of social accounting still receives a good deal of attention and we shall devote a chapter of this work to the discussion of the statistical measurement of changes in real product. But while historically, at least, studies of this sort have pride of place among those concerned with the description of economic activity in the aggregate, they have become absorbed by another, related, but wider, type of study which we must now consider.

### 3. *A simple system of national income accounts*

Studies of the national product are concerned with obtaining a measurement of the aggregate results of economic activity in a given period. A more recent development has been the statistical description of economic activity in such a way that the formation and disposal of national product is traced to the decisions of persons grouped in accordance with their functions. The complexities of the modern economy which result from the elaborate division of labour, and the use of money, make it difficult without some kind of statistical framework of this kind to assess even in rough quantitative terms the results of given political, business or personal activity in the aggregate.

In their simplest forms, as shown in this chapter, national income accounts are no more than measurements of production, consumption and investment arranged in such a way as to emphasise the distinction between the decisions of people concerned with, on the one hand, the production of commodities, and on the other the consumption of what has been produced. In a developed economy these are different groups of persons, though, of course, many people are members of both groups.

The reader at this stage may perhaps think that he is being asked to concern himself with trivialities, for, after all, it is fairly obvious that if you produce goods you have only two alternatives open: to consume them or not to consume them. For the following reasons, however, this view is probably unjustified. First, it is possible to under-estimate the importance of the *form* in which statements are made. By emphasising, in statistical terms, the dual nature of transactions attention is drawn to the possibility that, in the aggregate, the plans of consumers of commodities may be inconsistent with the plans of producers: this is of importance in relation to the study of problems of business fluctuations and economic policy generally. Secondly, analysis of the results of economic transactions in terms of the activities of *classes* of decision-makers (commonly called *transactors*) can, as will appear later in this book, be carried a good way beyond the simple example discussed in this chapter, the comprehension of which is only the first step towards the understanding of more complex systems.

In a certain sense the close connexion between the development of social accounting and the earlier concept of national product, or national income, has perhaps been unfortunate, for it has focused attention on one aspect of economic relationships—that relating to those, often rather vaguely defined, changes in the over-all value of the property of a person or group of persons which are commonly called income—at the cost of neglecting changes in the quantities of each kind of property held by such persons or groups (sometimes called changes in asset structure), and changes in individual commodity prices. The connexion between social accounts and the complex economic world of everyday life is, for this reason, somewhat harder to grasp than might otherwise be the case. (In Part III of this book an attempt is made to deal with part of this problem.)

National income accounts record, then: (*a*) the value of *production* in a given period, which in turn is the sum of sales by producers of goods and services to consumers—that is, of *consumption*—and the value of additions to national wealth—that is, of *investment*, gross or net—this sum being regarded as the measure of a 'flow of value' to producers, that is, an increase in their command over resources; (*b*) the value of command over resources 'flowing' to the factors of production during the same period, that is, of *income*; (*c*) certain other 'transfers' of command over resources representing net accretions to given groups of transactors though not passing in exchange for currently produced goods and services—for example, taxes, interest on government debt, and social security benefits. Command over resources is *not* in this context synonymous with *money*: it also includes command due to the ownership of non-money claims on others (such as book debts and securities) and goods. The accounts thus reflect flows of 'value' and thereby represent a fairly high degree of abstraction. The simple accounts we discuss in this chapter reflect, for example, the fact that a business man organising the production of commodities transfers purchasing power to owners of factors of production in exchange for their services. This purchasing power is usually, but not necessarily, in the form of *general* purchasing power, i.e. of money. Thus, at any given time payment may be owing to some factors of production, so that the flow of services from them has been counterbalanced by a flow of a non-money claim—in this case a debt—to them. This may later be converted into money, but the latter transaction (which reflects a change in asset structure of two groups of people) will not appear in the conventional form of national income account. Similarly, employees may (in countries where it is not illegal) be recompensed for their services by the transfer to them not of money but of goods. In these cases the factors have received what is called *income*, but not necessarily *money*. The business man himself, if he is an owner-manager, will, if he is successful, be rewarded for his services by profit and this is called *income*, though it is probable that at least part of his profit will be represented by an increase not in money but in claims on other people and/or in the value of goods of various kinds which the business owns.

Nevertheless, it is often convenient to think of national income accounts *as if* they reflected money flows. When, for example, income is transferred by, say, a business man, in the form of a debt owing to the income-receiver, we can pretend that money has been paid over, but that it has been immediately re-lent to the business man; similarly if the business man has a profit which he has not withdrawn from his business, we can write into the accounts an imaginary money withdrawal and assume that the money has been immediately re-lent to the business. Payments in kind to employees may similarly be regarded as money payments which the recipients must immediately spend on the purchase from the business of the goods or services in question. (In those cases where the determination of the income involves valuation—as with profit—these imaginary amounts will be, by their nature, a matter of estimation.) When the words 'receipts' and 'payments' are used in this book they should be understood to refer, strictly speaking, to *value* flows and not exclusively, except where the context clearly requires otherwise, to actual money flows. Until they have read Part III, readers may, however, find it easier to think in terms of money flows.

Our first step in drafting the accounts is to classify 'transactors' into two groups, called 'sectors', which may be labelled 'firms' and 'households', corresponding to the activities of 'production' and 'consumption'. Evidently, all persons concerned with production must also be consumers, though the reverse is not true. Our system thus does not involve an exclusive classification of *persons*, but of *activities*. 'Firms' are all organisations using the services of factors of production for the purpose of producing goods and services. Thus the activities of a private person operating on his own account, for example a doctor or lawyer, would, so far as his business was concerned, be classified under 'firms'. Similarly, a private person owning a house is, *in that capacity*, treated as a firm, hiring out his house to others or, if he is an owner-occupier, to himself in the capacity of consumer; in the latter case a notional rent is 'imputed'.[1] 'Households' are all persons or groups of persons—wage-earners, salary-earners, property owners, business men—receiving payment for services rendered by them to firms. (Business men paying themselves the profits of their firms are classified with 'households' in their capacity of income recipients.)

The figures can be arranged in various ways. The term 'accounts' in its strict sense implies in fact one particular way—that familiar to

[1] Logic demands a similar imputation for motor-cars, pianos, etc. Statistical difficulties rule this out!

accountants, which will be discussed shortly—but we use it here in the wider sense it has acquired in national income studies, namely of an organised arrangement of figures relating to the economic activity of a given region. One arrangement, in which the transactions of an economy can be neatly represented, is called a *matrix*: a rectangular arrangement of numbers or symbols. (The figures on the boards in London buses which indicate the fare from one place to another are arranged in a kind of matrix.) A matrix thus consists of a set of rows and columns of figures. Each row in the type of matrix used for social accounts contains the receipts of one sector or class of transactor and each column contains the payments of one sector, so that each sector has one row and one column, and the payments from one sector to another are shown in the space where the column of one and the row of the other cross one another. A very simple matrix might look like this:[1]

| Receipts by / Payments by | 1 Firms | 2 Households | 3 Total |
|---|---|---|---|
| *a* Firms | — | 100 | 100 |
| *b* Households | 100 | — | 100 |
| *c* Total | 100 | 100 | 200 |

This matrix states the rather trivial fact that, in a self-contained economy in which all commodities produced were at once consumed, total payments by 'households' on the purchase of commodities (called *expenditure*) would equal total receipts by firms in respect of the sale of commodities and that total payments by firms to households in respect of the purchase of services of factors of production, which include profits, would equal total receipts by households in respect of the sale of these services (called *income*). It also indicates that total expenditure would equal total income: this arises from the fact that the total of payments of income by firms is so defined as to be equal to total value of the product of firms—it must be noted that income includes profits—and since the whole product is consumed, total receipts of firms from sales must be equal to total value of product. But total receipts from sales is the

[1] Throughout this book the numbers used in accounts must be assumed to represent the money unit of the national region, for example, the £ sterling.

same as total expenditure. This proves our original statement. The numerical values of total 'income', total 'product' and total 'expenditure' are thus equal. In fact, each of these is so defined in national income studies that we really have not three different entities of the same size but three different *names* for the same numerical magnitude though, as we shall see, the distinction has relevance in relation to forecasts. When the region we are concerned with is that of a nation, it is customary to speak of 'national income', 'national expenditure' and 'national product'. In this example, though not, as we shall see in the next paragraph, in more complicated cases, the numerical value of 'expenditure' is also an index of the consumption of goods, which, as explained on page 12, are assumed to disappear once they have passed from the hands of firms into those of consumers.

The first step in the development of more complex examples is taken when we allow for the fact that part of the output of firms, in the creation of which incomes are paid to owners of factors of production, will normally not be sold as consumption goods, but will be acquired by other firms or retained by the same firms. This will include both capital equipment and stocks of raw materials, work in progress and finished goods held by firms, though in calculating this figure we must allow for decreases in stocks held at the beginning of the year. The value of this part of output is *net investment*, if depreciation is deducted, and *gross investment* if it is not. In all our examples we shall make no deduction for depreciation; accordingly national product or income will be expressed in gross terms. Now, by definition: (*a*) payments of income by firms are equal to receipts of income by households; (*b*) payments of income by firms are equal to the value of output (product) of firms; (*c*) receipts of firms from the sale of consumption goods to households *plus* the value of investment of firms equal the value of output of firms. It follows that the amount of receipts of income by households that is not spent on consumption goods—which is called *saving*—equals the value of investment by firms. This is the famous (to economists) 'ex-post' equality of savings and investment: 'ex-post' because it relates to a picture of transactions which have already taken place. (We shall refer to this equality again later in this chapter, when we discuss the symbolic statement of these relationships.)

In a very simple economy, like the one we are discussing, we can imagine that an amount equal to the receipts of income by households which are not spent on consumption is handed over by them to firms, thus enabling the latter to pay out to factors of production an amount equal to firms' investment. We have to remember, however, that in real life things are more complicated. Saving, like the other magnitudes we have discussed, is really not a quantity of money or of some other valuable thing. It is a *measurement*, and the savings-investment equality is really only a representation of the fact that if persons as a whole consume less than the output which they have created, resources are thereby made available for accumulation. The actual process of transfer of resources, or claims on resources, from savers to investors may be very complex. For a full understanding of the significance of the savings-investment equality we believe it is necessary to have some kind of mental picture of the asset structure of the economy and the changes therein. The discussion of this we have postponed to Part III.

The introduction of investment and saving into the accounts could be done by showing, in the firms sector, payments of income to factors in excess of receipts of expenditure on consumption from households, and similarly, in the households sector, receipts in excess of expenditure on consumption goods and services. This method will be used (for saving) in Part III. It is, however, convenient for some purposes to introduce a new row and a new column, to which we give the name 'capital'. We now show the amount of the saving of households as a 'payment' from households to capital, with an equal 'payment' by capital to firms for investment. The capital account thus symbolises the process of financing investment. Probably the best way of looking at it is as a convenient table for summarising, and in the more complex examples analysing, the sources of saving and the main classes of investment. It does not represent a functional sector of the economy in the same way that firms and households (and, as we shall see, government) do.[1]

If we assume that, of our original total income of 100, 20 is saved, or, in other words, of our original gross product of 100, 20 is gross investment, our matrix will now appear in the form shown on p. 21.

As already noted, firms' receipts (shown in row *a*) consist of (*a*) receipts from the sale of goods and services to households and (*b*) receipts for the finance of such additions to wealth as plant and machinery, or net increases in stocks of raw materials, finished goods or work-in-progress. Of course, individual firms may buy and sell

[1] Another method would be to have a 'capital' row and a 'capital' column for each sector. In this example households' saving would appear as a payment in the households' capital column, and firms' investment as a receipt in the firms' capital row. The other column and the other row would be empty. What we have here is a 'combined capital account'.

| Receipts by / Payments by | 1 Firms | 2 Households | 3 Capital | 4 Total |
|---|---|---|---|---|
| *a* Firms | — | 80 | 20 | 100[1] |
| *b* Households | 100 | — | — | 100[5] |
| *c* Capital | — | 20 | — | 20[3] |
| *d* Total | 100[2] | 100[6] | 20[4] | 220 |

[1] Gross national expenditure or product
[2] Gross national income or product
[3] Saving
[4] Gross investment
[5] Personal income
[6] Personal expenditure plus saving

from one another, but all these transactions (which in aggregate cancel out) are left out of account. If they were to be represented they would appear as a number in the space where the firms column intersects the firms row. For the time being all such transactions are ignored: in accounting terminology, the accounts for all firms are presented in 'consolidated' form.

Similarly the income received by households may, in aggregate, be devoted to two purposes: it may be spent on purchases of goods and services from firms for consumption, or it may be saved. Individual households may transfer purchasing power from one another by gift, but, as with firms, these transactions are omitted here: households' accounts are 'consolidated'.

The total of spending on (*a*) consumption and (*b*) investment—100 in this example, given by the total of row *a*—is still called gross expenditure and remains by definition equal to gross income, given by the total of column 1.

Thus, the investment figure of 20 in our example represents the addition to wealth which has resulted from the excess of the money value of production over the amount spent on consumption. This excess represents the value of additions to fixed equipment plus additions to or minus deductions from stocks of raw materials, work-in-progress and finished goods in the hands of producers. The calculation of investment is thus a process of valuation.

The profits of firms are defined as the difference between (*a*) the amounts receivable from sale of consumption goods, plus the value of investment, *less* (*b*) the amounts paid out as incomes to all factors of production *except* those entitled to the residuary share, whom we may call 'entrepreneurs'. This difference is the income of 'entrepreneurs'. In practice, of course, it is not usual for those in control of a business to distribute the whole of its profit in money—in many cases, indeed, it would only be possible to do so by borrowing, since the whole or part of the profit may be represented by rises in non-money assets. What we do is to transfer *conceptually* the whole of profits to the household sector, remembering that, to the extent that profits are in fact left in the business, they will be automatically saved and therefore conceptually transferred back to the firms sector as savings. Had, in our example, profits been higher by say 10, e.g. because end-year stocks were 10 higher, and there had been no other changes, then income 'payments' by firms and 'receipts' by households would both have been higher by 10, and so also would have been savings and investment. In other words, profits are part of households' income, whether distributed to owners or left in the relevant businesses: there is a 'flow of value' to households.

Our treatment here is in line with official practice with regard to unincorporated businesses. The undistributed profits of incorporated businesses, on the other hand, are treated as savings of the firms sector as shown in Chapter 2. For the purpose of this chapter we shall not make any accounting distinction between incorporated and unincorporated businesses.

We now turn to the form of presentation from which national income accounting derives the last word of its name. The presentation of national income data in account form parallels in some respects the double entry accounting methods of business. It is in this form that it has become customary for governments to publish the statistics of the main economic aggregates of their national economies. The matrix form has so far been used largely for the more detailed classifications to be discussed in the next section of this chapter.

When we set out the figures of our first matrix in account form we have something like this:

*Firms (Production)*

| *Receipts* | | | *Payments* | | |
|---|---|---|---|---|---|
| 1. (=4) | Sales of consumption goods and services to households | 100 | 2. (=3) | Purchases of factor services from households | 100 |
| | | 100 | | | 100 |

*Households (Consumption)*

| *Receipts* | | *Payments* | |
|---|---|---|---|
| 3. Sales of factor services to (=2) firms | 100 | 4. Purchases of consumption (=1) goods and services from firms | 100 |
| | 100 | | 100 |

In these accounts, figures on the left-hand side represent 'receipts', i.e. additions to the command over resources enjoyed by the group whose activities are shown in the account. Figures on the right-hand side represent 'payments', i.e. reductions in the command over resources. This arrangement is arbitrary, and is sometimes reversed. The single figure 100 in the matrix which represents payments by firms to households is represented by two figures in the account form, one in the account of firms (the payments side) and one in the account of households (the receipts side). It is exactly the same with the transactions in the reverse direction. Since each item is always represented twice, on opposite sides, the total of all entries on the left-hand side must always equal the total on the right-hand side. This provides an arithmetical check. Furthermore, if the item on one side is, in practice, derived from a different set of original statistical records from the equivalent item on the opposite side, an explicit check on statistical accuracy is provided by the fact that both must total to the same amount. This check can, of course, be applied where matrix form is used; nevertheless the double entry method provides a subtle reminder, which is absent in other systems, of the possibility of inaccuracy.

When we reproduce in account form the data from our second matrix we need an additional account to record the 'capital' transactions. (It will be noted that one account is needed for each row or column in the matrix.) The second set of figures will appear as follows:

*Firms (Production)*

| *Receipts* | | *Payments* | |
|---|---|---|---|
| 1. Sales of consumption (=5) goods and services to households | 80 | 3. Purchases of factor (=4) services from households | 100 |
| 2. Gross investment (=8) | 20 | | |
| | 100 | | 100 |

*Households (Consumption)*

| *Receipts* | | *Payments* | |
|---|---|---|---|
| 4. (=3) Sales of factor services to firms | 100 | 5. (=1) Purchases of consumption goods and services from firms | 80 |
| | | 6. (=7) Households' saving | 20 |
| | 100 | | 100 |

*Capital (Savings-Investment)*

| *Receipts* | | *Payments* | |
|---|---|---|---|
| 7. (=6) Households' saving | 20 | 8. (=2) Gross investment | 20 |
| | 20 | | 20 |

The arrangement of national income data in matrices or in accounts can be expressed in symbolic form. Thus the content of the households row and column in the second matrix, and of the households account in the second set of accounts, can be described by writing

$$Y = C + S$$

where

Y is total income (receipts from sales of factor services) = 100
C is expenditure on consumption (households' purchases of consumption goods and scrvices) = 80
S is saving (income of households not consumed) = 20

Similarly the content of the firms row and column and the firms account can be summed up by the statement

$$Y = C + I$$

where

Y is total income (payments by firms for factor services) = 100
C is expenditure on consumption (receipts by firms from sale of consumption goods and services) = 80
I is expenditure on investment (receipts by firms for the finance of additions to wealth which can also be interpreted as the value of the product of firms not sold for consumption) = 20.

It follows that S=I.

The above identities summarise in algebraic form the contents of our discussion on pages 19 and 20 above. The identity of S and I is the symbolic statement of the 'ex-post' equality of saving and investment already discussed. The use of the words 'saving' and 'investment' in this way for the same magnitude is, of course, a matter of choice and convenience. (Economists, like other people when they employ technical terms, make use of Humpty Dumpty's privilege of making words mean what they please. The meaning of the term 'saving' given here is not the only one which has been given to it.)

It is important to remember, however, that we are dealing with statistics of *realised* income and *realised* expenditure. *Intended* or *expected* income and expenditure for a given period, in the sense of the sum of individual expectations at the beginning of the period, may very well be unequal, as explained below in connexion with savings and investment. (It will, of course, never be possible to set an exact figure on the sum of the expectations of many people.) Which of the two words 'investment' or 'saving' will be used in a given context is, when we are concerned with the *past*, largely a matter of viewpoint. If one is thinking of the accumulation of wealth one may speak of 'investment'. If one is thinking of the exercise of thrift one may speak of 'saving'. The distinction between the two terms becomes important when we are thinking not of what has already happened but of *anticipations*; for the class of people that makes firms' decisions is not identical in all respects with the class that makes decisions to save. Hence *intended* saving may very well not be equal to *intended* investment (where by the quantity intended we again mean the sum of all individual intentions), even though prospective savers are thinking of savings as income received not consumed, and prospective investors are thinking of investment as income paid out not financed by sale of consumption goods and services, that is both are *defining* saving and investment as we are. What is *actually* saved or invested in this sense, however, will depend upon the *actual* level of income as well as on any individual changes of plan that occur. If intended investment and intended saving are not equal in total one or other or both sets of anticipations will be disappointed.

It is necessary here again to emphasise that national income accounts do *not* necessarily reflect *money* transactions but rather changes in the *command over resources* which may be in the form either of *claims* (including money) or goods. The acquisition of the right to receive a money payment is, for example, part of income even though the money has not yet been received. If we were to consider the flow of incomes in an economy for the period from Saturday to the following Tuesday, we should have to remember that though wage-earners would not, in general, by Tuesday night have been paid for the work done on Monday and Tuesday, yet the money *value* of wages 'earned' was part of their income (and, therefore, of income of households), and was regarded as an equivalent outlay by firms who would now possess the goods produced during these two days. In this case, since no money would have passed the amount due would be regarded as income *saved*—i.e. not yet used by the recipients to buy consumption goods—left by them with their firms as a temporary 'loan'. We could speak of a payment-out of income by firms; a receipt of income by households; an equivalent expenditure by households (saving) by way of temporary loan to firms; and a corresponding 'investment' by firms. This would be the formal way of expressing the fact that, until pay day, wage-earners would have found some of the finance for the production of goods or services. This is an illustration of the fundamental fact of life that when *any* goods or services are produced which are not immediately consumed *someone* has for the time being to forego consumption they could otherwise have enjoyed. Of course, the goods or services produced, or existing stocks of goods, might be consumed between Saturday and Tuesday, so that this saving by the owners of factors might, and probably would, be wholly or partly offset, in aggregate by their own, or someone else's simultaneous *dissaving*, instead of being balanced by investment.

In practice, in a long accounting period an account of actual money receipts and payments will in some respects (though not, for example, with respect to profits) give a fairly good approximation to income and expenditure. The theoretical distinction between money flows and income flows should, however, be understood. Let us see how the above transactions would be reflected in the accounts. First of all we have (*a*) the production of goods, in respect of which we record here as 'investment' that part of their value which the wages to be paid to the relevant work-people are assumed to measure, that is, we ignore 'value added' by other factors of production; (*b*) a 'flow' of income to the work-people represented by their claim for Monday's and Tuesday's wages, equal to (*a*). (If (*b*) is not regarded as equal to (*a*) either a loss or a profit has occurred from the point of view of the firm. We ignore this possibility here; but it must be remembered that any such profits or losses would be part of the income (positive or negative) of the entrepreneur in question, so that the value of production would still, by definition, equal total income, though the latter might, for example, be the resultant of positive wages and negative profits.) The flow of value to the firm which we call investment (it might, since it represents new products, be better regarded as a 'welling up' of value) is recorded as a 'receipt' of firms and the claim of the wage-earners as a 'payment' of firms. These are shown, using arbitrary figures, as follows:

*Firms*

| | | | |
|---|---|---|---|
| Investment in stocks | 50 | Purchases of factor services from work-people | 50 |

The increased claim of the work-people on the firm we show in households account as follows:

*Households*

| | |
|---|---|
| Sales of factor services to firm | 50 |

We also show the fact that the work-people have not yet spent their wages on consumption by inserting a 'payment' of 50 for saving (which in this very simple case does reflect a direct transfer of value from work-people to firms) so that our final households account is as follows:

*Households*

| | | | |
|---|---|---|---|
| Sales of factor services to firm | 50 | Saving, represented by non-spending on consumption of undrawn wages | 50 |

But now we must remember that the work-people or their wives will, during the two days in question, be spending money on food and clothing, etc. Let us assume that the total amount spent in this way (we are still ignoring, of course, all other people in the economy) is 45. Then, in the households sector we must show spending on consumption of that amount, so that the actual amount of saving is, net, only 5, though this 5 consists of two components, a saving of 50 of this week's wages less a dissaving of 45. Households account would then look like this:

*Households*

| | | | |
|---|---|---|---|
| Sales of factor services | 50 | Saving | 50 |
| Dissaving | 45 | Purchase of consumption goods | 45 |

Or, putting dissaving and saving together:

| | *Households* | | |
|---|---|---|---|
| Sales of factor services | 50 | Purchase of consumption goods | 45 |
| | | Saving | 5 |
| | 50 | | 50 |

The spending on consumption goods will probably not go to the actual firm, that is employing these people, but to other firms. These will sell goods and, ignoring all other transactions, that is, assuming they have no concurrent production, will be receiving payments for the goods and be disinvesting by reducing their stocks. If we put the accounts of these firms and of the original firm together, they might look like this:

| | *Firms* | | |
|---|---|---|---|
| Investment in stocks | 50 | Purchases of factor services | 50 |
| Sales to households | 45 | Disinvestment in stocks | 45 |

In the aggregate account, however, the sale out of stocks in some firms would be offset against the increase in stocks in others, so that we should have:

| | *Firms* | | |
|---|---|---|---|
| Investment in stocks | 5 | Purchases of factor services | 50 |
| Sales to households | 45 | | |
| | 50 | | 50 |

Readers may imagine for themselves other transactions. When all the figures for the economy are put together we have our national income accounts. (In the case of the production of services, of course, there can be no building up of stocks.)

The flows of 'value' which we call 'income' and 'expenditure' are thus a highly abstract way of describing in aggregate the complex activity of the economy. The picture so obtained is, like all abstractions, lacking in many essential details and must be used with care. Some of the problems will be discussed later. (One which may be mentioned here is the fact that changes in the general price level must be allowed for before national income figures in terms of money values can reflect even reasonably approximately the equivalent flows of real goods and services.)

It will be clear to those with some knowledge of economics that though the basic ideas of production, consumption, investment, saving, are very old indeed the system we have been discussing owes very much to a work which has had great influence on the development of social accounting, the late Lord Keynes's *The General Theory of Employment, Interest and Money*, published in 1936. One of Lord Keynes's contributions was to set out the relationships between the various aggregates in a way that gave a great impetus to thought in this field.

The particular arrangements in matrix and account form described above are not the only way of illustrating these concepts. Another way of picturing the general ideas we have discussed is to use some kind of 'flow diagram' in which the movement of money value in the economy is represented pictorially. Diagrams of this type can sometimes help one to visualise more clearly some of the relationships between different sectors of the economy. Flow diagrams had been used in various forms in many works published before the *General Theory*, though interest tended to attach more to the demonstration of the distribution of the separate flows of income among classes of recipients and the distribution of expenditure among different goods and services, than to the measurement of the components of the main aggregates: production, consumption and accumulation (or investment) discussed in the preceding section.

National income accounting is largely a combination and development of earlier ideas to a stage in which the accounts are able to picture a little more clearly the complexities of everyday life and provide some guide to orders of magnitude.

Whether matrix or account form or any other method of presentation is used in any particular case for the purpose of exhibiting the kind of economic magnitude we are discussing is a matter entirely of convenience in handling the figures and presenting them clearly to the reader. The meaning of the figures inserted remains the same in all cases. On the other hand, the method of arrangement is not unimportant, for one method may be better adapted to conveying an overall picture of relationships inside the economy. The matrix form economises space, since only one entry is required where in the case of account form two are needed. On the other hand, double-entry systems have at least one advantage: they provide a useful automatic check on accuracy of arithmetic and completeness of data. Moreover, they are familiar to business men.

The clear-cut distinction between the two methods of presentation is only evident when they are used to present an *over-all* picture of the economy. In practice, of course, many of the figures given in official publications and elsewhere represent only *sections* of the economy, and hence often no question arises of setting them out in a form in which the inter-relations with other sections are made explicit. In such cases any convenient tabular presentation may be used.

4. *Input-output accounts*

For certain purposes we may be interested in the classification of output by industrial classes, that is, we may wish to examine separately the value of the final output of manufactures, agriculture, transport services and so on. Moreover, we may be interested in what is going on within the firms sector of the economy. Industries sell to one another as well as to final consumers.

Let us consider a very simple economy with only two industries which we shall call 'manufacturing' and 'other'. These industries sell part of their product to households and part to one another as raw material.

For instance, 'other' (which includes agriculture) may sell fruit directly to consumers, but also sell it to 'manufacturing' for jam making. In the first case, the fruit is part of what is called 'final output'. In the second, the 'output' is not final, for it is in turn an 'input' of 'manufacturing' contributing to the manufacture of jam which is a 'final output' of 'manufacturing'. Similarly, 'manufacturing' may sell coal to households for everyday use, but sell it to 'other' for heating greenhouses or cowsheds in winter, in which case it is an 'input'. (Final 'outputs' might be called 'inputs' of households: but it is usual to call these 'consumption'.)

That this type of analysis is merely a development, through more detailed classification, of the type of classification described in the previous section can be shown by considering the matrix on page 21. The heading 'firms' covers both 'manufacturing' and 'other', each of which sells to the other one, their transactions being eliminated in the matrix. If we wished we could insert in the space where the firms column and the firms row intersect the value of all inter-industry sales. If we wanted, however, to distinguish receipts and payments of 'manufacturing' from those of 'other' we should have to subdivide the firms row and column as shown in the following, amended, matrix:

| Receipts by \ Payments by | | 1 Firms: Manu-facturing | 1 Firms: Other | 2 Households | 3 Capital | 4 Total |
|---|---|---|---|---|---|---|
| *a* Firms | Manufac-turing | — | 10 | 40 | 10 | 60 |
| | Other | 15 | — | 40 | 10 | 65 |
| *b* Households | | 45 | 55 | — | — | 100 |
| *c* Capital | | — | — | 20 | — | 20 |
| *d* Total | | 60 | 65 | 100 | 20 | 245 |

This indicates that 'other' bought 'inputs' valued at 10 from 'manufacturing' and that 'manufacturing' bought 'inputs' valued at 15 from 'other'. The other figures are unchanged in total, but receipts of households and capital accounts are now divided into receipts from 'manufacturing' and receipts from 'other', and likewise with payments.

Total receipts of firms, shown in the two sub-divisions of row *a*, are now 60+65=125, compared with 100 in the original matrix. This is because we show the receipts of each group of firms from the other group, as well as the receipts by each group of what is called 'final expenditure', that is, expenditure on consumption (shown in the households column) and on investment (shown in the capital column). Similarly, total payments of firms, shown in the two sub-divisions of column 1, now include inter-group payments, and sum likewise to 125. Gross national expenditure remains 100, given by the difference between total receipts of firms, 125, and inter-firm payments, 25. Gross national income is derived in the same way by deducting inter-firm payments from total payments of firms. Both results are, as we know, equivalent to gross national product.

The aggregates to which the names gross national 'expenditure', 'product' and 'income' are given can thus be derived from the more elaborate table by removing those items which, because they are only a transfer between firms inside a sector, and do not therefore represent an addition to resources available for consumption or investment, are excluded from the aggregates. In our simple example we merely have to ignore inter-firm transfers in column 1 and row *a* and the resultant totals of the row and column will yield up the figures we need, just as they were derived on page 21.

The statement that inter-firm transfers do not add to national resources means merely that once a firm has processed the resources passed to it, which forms its inputs—and 'processing' covers transporting over space and time as well as changes in form—the mere handing over of legal ownership and control to another firm is not considered to add to value. Another reason for the cancellation of inter-form transfers is that thereby a simpler picture of the economy can be presented than would otherwise be possible. On the other hand the picture then becomes, necessarily, somewhat less adequate as a description of the activity of the whole economy.

It would be easy enough to convert our more elaborate matrix into double-entry account form. All that we should have to do would be to insert two accounts or sectors, for 'manufacturing' and 'other', where formerly we had only one for 'firms'; or we could show separately the transactions of both industries in one account. The more we sub-divide, however, the more unwieldy does account form become, and the relatively more convenient the matrix form.

For the purpose of studying inter-industry relationships we can obviously select the corner of the matrix which relates only to 'firms'. A fairly complete picture of real life inter-industry relations would, of course, occupy a very large area of paper, depending upon how detailed the classifications were made. In the ultimate analysis each individual business could, in theory, be given a row and a column. (In the same way, the other sectors could similarly, in theory, be sub-classified until each decision-maker in the economy had a row and a column for each class of decisions he made.)

This so-called 'input-output' approach to social accounting is associated with the name of Wassily Leontief who constructed a matrix for the whole United States economy in his now famous work *The Structure of American Economy, 1919–1929*, which first appeared in 1941, some five years after Keynes's *General Theory*. We shall discuss this further in Chapter 8.

followed shortly afterwards by home disinvestment and simultaneous overseas investment. However, although for some purposes the intermediate stages may be of interest, when we are concerned with the net effect of transactions in a given period these can be ignored.

2. *Accounting for overseas transactions*

Perhaps the simplest way of showing the implications of overseas transactions, and how they are dealt with in the accounts, is to consider typical situations *in vacuo*, so to speak, that is, as if no other transactions had taken place in the economy. Let us first take the export of newly created goods and services. We have to consider the processes of (*a*) creating the goods or services and (*b*) permitting the overseas customer to assume control over them. The corresponding flows of value shown in the accounts will be: (*a*) payment of incomes (including profit) to the factors of production for their services in creating the commodities, and (*b*) receipt from the overseas customer of payment for them.

The first part of the transaction will be recorded like this:

*Firms*

| | | | |
|---|---|---|---|
| | | Purchases of factor services from households | 10 |

*Households*

| | | | |
|---|---|---|---|
| Sales of factor services to firms | 10 | | |

We have not, however, yet recorded the 'flow of value' represented by the receipt by firms of money or some other claim from the overseas customer. If we insert this we have:

*Firms*

| | | | |
|---|---|---|---|
| Sales of goods and services to non-residents | 10 | Purchases of factor services from households | 10 |

Finally, symmetry is preserved in the accounts by showing, as before, a 'payment' from households equal to the income they have saved, so that we have:

*Households*

| | | | |
|---|---|---|---|
| Sales of factor services to firms | 10 | Households' saving | 10 |

# 2

# NATIONAL INCOME ACCOUNTS: TRANSACTIONS WITH THE REST OF THE WORLD

## 1. *Imports and exports*

We now return to the simple system of national income accounts which we discussed in section 3 of Chapter 1. So far our hypothetical economy has had no relations with other economies at all. An obvious next stage in our analysis, therefore, is to examine what happens when we introduce transactions with people and organisations not ordinarily resident in the national region.

Let us assume that firms have transactions with the outside world and that they buy imports of raw materials from non-residents and sell finished goods abroad. From the point of view of their effect on the economy these transactions are very similar to the investment transactions of firms which we discussed in Chapter 1. Let us take as an example the effect of exports. In whatever way the overseas customer pays, the result must (unless the export is a free gift) be an improvement in the overseas wealth of the home country. Either the non-resident must transfer gold or overseas currency or some other asset to the home country; or he must surrender a bank balance or some other asset he already has there, thus reducing the claims of non-residents as a whole on the home country; or he must borrow in the home country (either at short or longer term) thus increasing the claims of the latter on the rest of the world. Whether or not the overseas investment represented by an export is a *net* increase in the wealth of the exporting country in a given period depends upon whether it arises from newly created wealth or is a sale from existing stocks. In the latter case there will be simultaneous domestic dis-investment. Indeed, even when newly created goods are exported this can, if one chooses, be regarded as a process of domestic investment followed shortly afterwards by home disinvestment and simultaneous overseas investment. However, although for some purposes the intermediate stages may be of interest, when we are concerned with the net effect of transactions in a given period these can be ignored.

2. *Accounting for overseas transactions*

Perhaps the simplest way of showing the implications of overseas transactions, and how they are dealt with in the accounts, is to consider typical situations *in vacuo*, so to speak, that is, as if no other transactions had taken place in the economy. Let us first take the export of newly created goods and services. We have to consider the processes of (*a*) creating the goods or services and (*b*) permitting the overseas customer to assume control over them. The corresponding flows of value shown in the accounts will be: (*a*) payment of incomes (including profit) to the factors of production for their services in creating the commodities, and (*b*) receipt from the overseas customer of payment for them.

The first part of the transaction will be recorded like this:

*Firms*

| | | | |
|---|---|---|---|
| | | Purchases of factor services from households | 10 |

*Households*

| | | | |
|---|---|---|---|
| Sales of factor services to firms | 10 | | |

We have not, however, yet recorded the 'flow of value' represented by the receipt by firms of money or some other claim from the overseas customer. If we insert this we have:

*Firms*

| | | | |
|---|---|---|---|
| Sales of goods and services to non-residents | 10 | Purchases of factor services from households | 10 |

Finally, symmetry is preserved in the accounts by showing, as before, a 'payment' from households equal to the income they have saved, so that we have:

*Households*

| | | | |
|---|---|---|---|
| Sales of factor services to firms | 10 | Households' saving | 10 |

economy, so that the significance of the entries in the accounts can be thrown up more clearly.

Suppose that the only transactions in the economy were exports of goods which formed part of stocks at the beginning of our accounting period. How would these enter into the accounts? There is now no transaction with households. Only one sector is concerned: firms. We can record a receipt by firms from non-residents in payment for the export. At the same time we must record the amount of the disinvestment in stock, so that we have:

*Firms*

| | | | |
|---|---|---|---|
| Sales of goods to non-residents | 10 | Disinvestment in stocks | 10 |

What about the rest of the world and the capital account? There has been no net saving, either by firms or by households. Are any entries necessary? The answer to this is that though there has been no net investment or saving, there has been a change in the form of investment, which it is convenient to record in the capital account. Accordingly we record the export in the rest of the world account, and show the disinvestment in stocks in the capital account, which gives us:

*Rest of the world*

| | | | |
|---|---|---|---|
| | | Purchases of exports from firms by non-residents | 10 |

*Capital*

| | | | |
|---|---|---|---|
| Disinvestment in stocks | 10 | | |

We can now indicate in capital account the amount of investment abroad, 'summarised' for us in the rest of the world account, the value of which is given by the balancing item in the latter which we insert as a 'receipt', so that we have:

*Rest of the world*

| | | | |
|---|---|---|---|
| Net investment abroad | 10 | Purchases of exports from firms by non-residents | 10 |

*Capital*

| | | | |
|---|---|---|---|
| Disinvestment in stocks | 10 | Net investment abroad | 10 |

The accounting for imports runs exactly parallel with that for exports except that, of course, imports represent disinvestment abroad and increase correspondingly the resources available internally for consumption, domestic investment or exports. The home country can pay for imports by transferring gold or overseas money balances which it already possesses, or by transferring other overseas assets (such as securities in overseas enterprises), or by borrowing, that is, transferring claims against its own government or residents, short or long term, ranging from money balances (bank deposits in the home country) to long-term government loans.

We shall now extend the accounts discussed in Chapter 1 to deal with overseas transactions. We shall then show the same data in matrix form and finally indicate, by extending our set of algebraic identities, how the new relationships can be shown in symbolic form. We shall end the chapter by examining a little more closely the nature of transactions introduced into the accounts under the names 'exports' and 'imports'.

### 3. *The whole system of accounts with overseas transactions*

In drawing up our extended system of accounts we shall introduce arbitrary figures for exports and imports. As we wish, for demonstration purposes, to arrive at the same figure for gross national product as before we shall have to alter arbitrarily some of the magnitudes used in section 3 of Chapter 1. Let us assume that exports are 10 and imports 12, so that overseas disinvestment is 2, consumption 82, gross domestic investment 20 as before. We will also take this opportunity of bringing the accounts a little closer to current practice by assuming that while 'payments' for factor services remain at 100, 10 of this amount is the undistributed profit of corporate business. This is shown as saving in firms account, leaving 90 'paid' to households. (This has, of course, nothing to do with the introduction of overseas transactions.) We shall find that the net effect of these changes is to bring households' saving down to 8, and total saving (that is, including saving of 10 by corporate business in the firms sector) to 18. We then have:

*Firms*

| | *Receipts* | | | *Payments* | |
|---|---|---|---|---|---|
| 1. (=8) | Sales of consumption goods and services to households | 82 | 4. (=7) | Purchases of factor services from households | 90 |
| 2. (=16) | Gross domestic investment | 20 | 5. (=10) | Purchases of imports from non-residents | 12 |
| 3. (=11) | Sales of exports to non-residents | 10 | 6. (=13) | Firms' saving | 10 |
| | | 112 | | | 112 |

*Households*

| Receipts | | | Payments | | |
|---|---|---|---|---|---|
| 7. (=4) | Sales of factor services to firms | 90 | 8. (=1) | Purchases of consumption goods and services from firms | 82 |
| | | | 9. (=14) | Households' saving | 8 |
| | | 90 | | | 90 |

*Rest of the world*

| Receipts | | | Payments | | |
|---|---|---|---|---|---|
| 10. (=5) | Sales of imports to firms | 12 | 11. (=3) | Purchases of exports from firms | 10 |
| | | | 12. (=15) | Net disinvestment abroad | 2 |
| | | 12 | | | 12 |

*Capital*

| Receipts | | | Payments | | |
|---|---|---|---|---|---|
| 13. (=6) | Firms' saving | 10 | 16. (=2) | Gross domestic investment | 20 |
| 14. (=9) | Households' saving | 8 | | | |
| 15. (=12) | Net disinvestment abroad | 2 | | | |
| | | 20 | | | 20 |

Our accounts now give a rather fuller picture of economic events in the national region. From them we can also derive the numerical magnitudes discussed in section 2 of Chapter 1 which summarise in a rough way these events. The magnitude of our gross national income is still identified with the sum of incomes of factors of production (items 4 and 6), which now include undistributed profit of firms, that is 100. This magnitude can equally well be derived by adding together the expenditure items, which, it will be remembered from Chapter 1, comprise consumption and investment, the latter now being the algebraic sum of domestic investment and overseas investment. Overseas investment is given by the difference between exports and imports. (In forms of account designed to emphasise the magnitudes we are discussing, the net difference of exports and imports is, in fact, grouped with domestic investment, as we shall see later.) Hence gross national expenditure is given by the sum of items 1, 2, 3, *less* item 5. It is, of course, 100.

The derivation of these magnitudes can be seen clearly if we convert our accounts into matrix form, using, as before, one row and one column for each account. (We indicate in the spaces of the matrix the code numbers of the corresponding items in the accounts.) For each figure in the matrix there are, of course, two figures in the accounts, but in drafting the matrix we treat the difference between payment by firms for imports and receipts by them for exports as a negative receipt, corresponding to the idea of disinvestment, and show transactions with the rest of the world as a single, net figure. This is a matter of arithmetical convenience, just like showing domestic investment net of any stock decreases. (We do this so that we can derive the magnitude of gross national product, etc., from the total of a single row and column.)

We then have:

| Receipts by / Payments by | 1<br>Firms | 2<br>House-holds | 3<br>Rest of the World | 4<br>Capital | 5<br>Total |
|---|---|---|---|---|---|
| *a*<br>Firms | — | 82<br>[1=8] | −2<br>[(3−5)=(11−10)] | 20<br>[2=16] | 100 |
| *b*<br>Households | 90<br>[4=7] | — | — | — | 90 |
| *c*<br>Rest of the World | — | — | — | −2<br>[15=12] | −2 |
| *d*<br>Capital | 10<br>[6=13] | 8<br>[9=14] | — | — | 18 |
| *e*<br>Total | 100 | 90 | −2 | 18 | 206 |

By totalling row *a* we arrive at the figure of 100 from the aspect of gross national expenditure, while column 1 gives the same figure from the aspect of gross income. The total of row *b* we call *personal* income (since it excludes that part of income which forms corporate savings in the firms sector), while column 2 gives the total of personal expenditure and personal saving, which is necessarily the same magnitude as personal income. The total of row *c* may be regarded as the net receipt from the rest of the world in respect of international transactions on current account, or the 'balance of payments on current account'. In this instance it is negative. The total of column 3 may be interpreted as net investment abroad, here a negative item. The total of row *d* shows the sum of home saving while the total of column 4 shows gross domestic investment (or capital formation) *less* disinvestment abroad.

We can restate the relationship between the magnitudes in the accounts in symbolic form. Our first identity in Chapter 1 was

$$Y = C + S.$$

S, however, is now divided into firms' (corporate) saving and households' saving. Let us call these $S_f$ and $S_h$ and write

$$S_f + S_h = S$$

so that

$$Y = C + S_f + S_h \tag{1}$$

or in figures

$$100 = 82 + 10 + 8.$$

Again, on page 24, we had

$$Y = C + I.$$

Using X to denote exports and M to denote imports, while I continues to denote gross domestic investment, we can now write

$$Y = C + I + X - M \tag{2}$$

or in figures

$$100 = 82 + 20 + 10 - 12.$$

It follows from (1) and (2) that

$$S_f + S_h = I + X - M$$

or in figures

$$10 + 8 = 20 + (-2)$$

which is a restatement of the savings-investment equality. (It is perhaps desirable at this point to remind readers familiar with the well-known Keynesian identities that in our present scheme Y is gross income since we ignore depreciation.)

4. *Further considerations*

Before we leave overseas transactions we must examine a little more closely the nature of the activities comprehended under the heads of 'exports' and 'imports'. These include not only transactions in goods, but such 'invisible' transactions as the sale or purchase of insurance cover, banking services, shipping facilities, etc., to or from residents in the rest of the world. 'Exports' also includes receipts from such transactions as the sale of goods and services to visitors from overseas, which give rise to claims in favour of the home country as surely as the direct dispatch of goods to territories abroad, while in the same way, expenditure by residents when they go abroad is equivalent to imports. Similarly we regard rents, interest and dividends currently receivable from abroad as part of the national income of the home country and group such receipts with exports, while payments in the reverse direction are classed with imports. This may be clearer if we think of receipts of rent, interest and dividends from abroad as the sale of the current services of the investment in respect of which they are paid. (In economic jargon, the income from overseas property may be regarded as a receipt from the sale of the services of 'waiting', 'sacrifice of liquidity' and 'uncertainty bearing'.)

It is thus convenient to include in our firms sector the activities of people in their capacity of holders of overseas property, the amount of the income being recorded as a receipt. A corresponding payment of 'factor income' to households is shown. Similar payments in the reverse direction are regarded as negative factor income and 'imports' of firms. This procedure allows us to pass through the firms account all receipts and payments that, by definition, go into the calculation of the national income and national product.[1] Exceptions, however, are sometimes made to the rule that transactions increasing or decreasing wealth abroad are passed through the firms account: these relate to receipts and payments—'remittances'—which arise from gifts passing between residents and non-residents and 'capital' transactions. We shall defer discussion of these to the next chapter, in which we turn to the activities of government.

[1] What is called the gross *domestic* product, on the other hand, excludes net income on overseas investments.

# 3

# NATIONAL INCOME ACCOUNTS: GOVERNMENT ACTIVITY

## 1. *The definition of government*

No description of a developed economy would be complete without some reference to the activities of the sovereign body. Whether this is a democratically-elected legislature or a dictatorship, and whether or not it elects to leave the process of production and distribution in private hands, it will influence and control in many respects the way in which resources of the community are utilised.

For social accounting purposes we can state as a first approximation that the government is a collective 'person' that purchases goods and services from firms in order to provide services which normally it does not sell and which, in its own judgment (it must be presumed), it can provide more conveniently or efficiently than private enterprise. These purchases may be financed by the compulsory withdrawal of purchasing power from private consumers, that is by taxation, or by government borrowing. This definition requires amplification, however.

First of all, it must be noted that we include in the term 'government' not only the central authority, but also local authorities and such agencies of the central authority as the social security funds administration. (These are sometimes called, collectively, the public authorities.) The financial relations between most government authorities is close, and the division of services between them is often a matter of convention. Thus the social security funds, although recorded in separate financial accounts, may be partially financed by government grants, and the contributions paid by employers and employees may, because they are compulsory, be regarded as taxes. For some purposes it would be useful to distinguish the activities of the separate public authorities, but lack of space prevents this here. Accordingly, in our accounts there will be no record of all the flows of income and expenditure between these authorities. Central government grants to local authorities and to social security funds, for example, and transfers from these agencies to central government, like transfers between households, will not appear.

The inclusion of social security agencies suggests a modification in our definition. We have defined the government as a collective 'person' that purchases goods and services from firms. However, social security payments generally take the form of money benefits and not the form of the provision of real services. In other words, the government may redistribute claims on the national product through its power to tax, but not necessarily in the form of goods and services in kind. The same is true in the case of payments of interest on the national debt—there is a redistribution of claims from taxpayers to fundholders. The general term for this form of expenditure is *transfer payments*. These, unlike payments for services of factors of production, are not regarded as made in respect of newly created services; they represent redistribution of income. It should be noted, however, that net government receipts or payments to *non-residents* do not represent redistribution of domestic income but are regarded as additions to or deductions from aggregate national income.

Again, our definition states that the government provides collective services 'which normally it does not sell'. A strict interpretation of this statement would mean the exclusion of all productive activity from the government sector. Now, in many countries the government owns or effectively controls a considerable part of 'productive' enterprise in the form of public utilities, the ownership of lands and buildings and, sometimes, other industries. The question arises, therefore, as to whether it is more convenient to regard such undertakings as part of the activity of the government sector or not. In so far as we wish to identify the firms sector with the production activities of the economy, it is appropriate to classify these undertakings as firms. In fact, many of these government enterprises, including nationalised undertakings, operate very much like private firms in that their costs of production are (or are intended to be) covered by those benefiting directly from the services that they provide. Furthermore, they usually have separate legal existence and financial independence, the latter characteristic being reflected in the power to maintain their own reserves and to borrow. From the point of view of classification by types of decision-maker this last characteristic is important, and it may be invoked as the main criterion to be used in deciding whether or not to regard a particular public enterprise as a corporate enterprise or as a government trading activity, though both types of enterprise may be classified with firms. Thus in the United Kingdom the main nationalised industries—National Coal Board, British Railways Board, and others—are regarded as 'corporate enterprises' while public enterprises such as the Post Office and local authority trading services are not, on the grounds that any trading surplus reverts to the Exchequer or to the local authorities. The distinction made in the United Kingdom national income accounts between the two types of public enterprise is very like the distinction between corporate and non-corporate business. Surplus income of corporate public enterprises, that is, profits not paid out in interest on capital, is, like undistributed company profits, treated as saving of firms, while on the other hand all the profits of non-corporate public enterprise are recorded as payments to the government sector, just as all profits of non-corporate private business are regarded as income of households. (The United States national income accounts, on the other hand, treat surpluses of *all* public enterprises as 'taxation' paid to government.)

### 2. *The classification of Government purchases*

The government sector may thus be regarded as delimiting a special section of the consumption activities of the economy in which purchases of goods and services are made on behalf of the community as a whole, taxes are received and certain transfer payments are made. We might thus regard the government as a special kind of 'household' whose activities are sufficiently different from those of other households to require separate classification. Productive activities of government, on the other hand, are classified in our system of accounts, like those of private persons, with firms. This, however, raises the question: what do we mean by the *productive* activities of government? These clearly include the various types of public corporation and trading body just discussed. Are there others?

The traditional functions of government are the preservation of law and order and the defence of the country from external attack. These functions presuppose the purchase by the government of the services of individuals as policemen, soldiers and administrators and the purchase of goods such as weapons of all kinds, aircraft, ships and so on.

Now, it will be remembered that in Chapter 1 we stated that interest in the concept of the national product and related aggregates was stimulated by the wish to find a suitable index of 'economic welfare'. Are all services, then, part of the national product, considered as such an index? Do they represent the creation of wealth that is then absorbed in satisfying the wants of consumers? Some economists, notably Professor Kuznets, are very doubtful about this. As he puts it,

> national income is a measure of net output . . . *within* the given social framework, not of what it would be in a hypothetical absence of the latter. The maintenance and modification of this framework . . . cannot in itself constitute part of the final product of economic activity. One could, if one wished, classify this social framework as a kind of basic capital, but not in the strict sense of economic capital whose increase and decrease can in and of itself enter economic accounting and national income. . . .
>
> In other words, the flow of services to individuals from the economy is a flow of economic goods produced and secured under conditions of internal peace, external safety, and legal protection of specific rights, and cannot include these very conditions as services. . . . There is little sense in talking of protection of life and limb as an economic service to individuals—it is a precondition of such services, not a service in itself.[1]

Professor Kuznets would therefore exclude all expenditure on law and order and defence from the national product aggregate on the grounds that they are its necessary prerequisites and not part of the product itself. With such a definition of national product only services of the government which had their counterpart in private markets, for example, the provision of rail transport, would be included in the aggregate.

We do not propose to do any more than state the problem here. It obviously makes a great deal of difference in any comparison of the real national product (i.e. the national product adjusted for any price level changes) over time or between regions whether government purchases of this kind are included or not. Consider any estimate of the real national product of the United Kingdom between, say, 1938 and 1948. The time period included six years of war, during which a large part of the resources of the nation were devoted to war purposes. This meant shortages of consumer goods and services of all kinds so that the nation as a whole was worse off in any ordinary sense of the words. Yet this observation would not

[1] Simon Kuznets, 'Government Product and National Income', *Income and Wealth*, series 1, pp. 193–4 (Bowes and Bowes, Cambridge).

be supported statistically if we regarded expenditure on arms and armies as alternative forms of 'consumption', so that the value of these items appeared as part of the national 'product'.

The case we have chosen is perhaps a rather extreme example and in more normal conditions the borderline between these two alternative ways of looking at government purchases is difficult to draw. Perhaps the most convincing argument in favour of regarding such government activity as contributing to the national product is that this gives us a better view of the total resources that are available, whatever use they may have been put to. If, then, we wish to draw attention to the fact that a large part of the nation's annual 'production' is represented by government activity, we have only to point to the classifications inside the framework of the accounts that record the expenditure of different sectors. In practice, statisticians treat all government purchases as entering into the calculation of gross national product.

Given this treatment, how are the accounts drafted? There is no difficulty where the goods and services bought by government have been produced by domestic business, the activities of which fall obviously into the firms account. The purchases by government are reflected in that account as sales of firms. Any purchases by government from abroad must also be passed through the firms account if that account is to record the disinvestment abroad caused by those purchases: for this purpose the activity of the government as an importer is classed with firms. In the same way any government activities resulting in the sale of goods and services abroad are classed with firms, even if they are not performed by government trading bodies in the literal sense. Similarly, the purchases by the government of services from its civil servants and members of the armed forces are regarded as a purchase from firms who pay out equivalent amounts as factor incomes. An alternative way of looking at this is to regard all government departments and agencies, civil and military, as firms 'selling' to the central government services valued at the same figures as the sum of the incomes they pay out to their employees *plus* purchases of goods and services from other firms and from abroad *less* sales abroad, if any. (The purchases from other firms will cancel out in the aggregate firms account against the sales of those firms.) Receipts of households from sales of factor services to firms will now include salaries, wages and pay of all government servants, including officers and men of the armed forces. In thus putting all these activities into the firms account we are only extending the list given in Chapter 1, where, the reader will remember, we explained how the activities of professional men, house owners, and so on are classified as 'productive' and recorded in the firms account.

This method of classification, which must be used if firms account is to record all 'productive' activity, reduces the activities recorded in the government sector to those of a kind of 'being' with two main functions: (*a*) that of buying various goods and services that are then applied for the benefit of the community and (*b*) redistributing income through taxation and transfer payments. (Activity (*a*) may also, of course, represent redistribution of income through the provision of collective benefits not distributed in proportion to the taxes which finance them.)

In the case of private persons it is the convention, as we explained in Chapter 1, to regard all purchases from firms as consumption,[1] even in those cases where the goods bought are likely to continue to provide services over a relatively long period, as is the case when such goods as motor-cars or pianos are bought. This is purely a matter of statistical convenience which does some injury to the value of the accounts as a picture of the economy. (This is particularly serious in periods when households are building up or running down stocks of durable goods on a large scale, since such action may have important implications for industrial activity, the level of imports, and so on, in the near future.) When we consider the activities of government we find that although, as we have mentioned, government can be regarded as a kind of collective person, a distinction is in fact made between current government expenditure, analogous with the consumption of households, and expenditure on 'capital' goods and on stock increases or decreases which in households we lump in with consumption goods.

The main reason for making this distinction is that public capital expenditure is nowadays on a very heavy scale—it includes outlays on schools, roads, publicly owned housing estates, and so on. It would be misleading to regard expenditure of this kind as belonging to the same class as government outlays on currently used goods and services. Much of it is very similar to business investment: if, for example, a political decision were made to pass the provision of schools and housing back to private enterprise, all expenditures of this kind would be recorded as investment in the 'private sector' from which factor incomes in the form of rent and profit would flow for many years. (A similar argument could be used, it is true, with respect to the households sector: the value of a motor-car, the pur-

[1] It will be remembered that houses are an exception.

chase of which by a private person is regarded as consumption, would be regarded as part of investment if it were bought by a firm carrying on the business of car-hiring.) Hence government expenditure which is regarded as representing 'capital formation', that is investment, will be dealt with in the accounts as investment in the production (firms) sector. The value of this capital formation is recorded as part of the investment item in the firms account, and no record of this appears in the government account, which, like households, records only 'current' expenditure.

Reflection will show that there is no essential difference in this respect in the *accounting* treatment of government and households: in both cases the problem is that of selecting the criterion which is applied in deciding which expenditures shall be treated as capital. In the case of households we saw that the holding of a house was regarded as a productive activity, from which it follows that even the value of a house built by a private person for himself would be part of investment, and would enter into the firms account. In the case of government, the data available may allow the category of activities regarded as investment to be rather wider than with private persons.

The division between government expenditure which is regarded as current and that which is considered to be capital formation is an arbitrary one. Obviously, the services of civil servants and the armed forces can be regarded as part of current expenditure because, in Adam Smith's phrase, they 'perish in the very instant of their performance', while, on the other hand, roads and hospitals and schools last for many years during which they provide services. But there are some categories of expenditure which present difficulties. For instance, expenditure on the building of battleships and barrack could be regarded as investment in the sense we have defined it. Are we to regard it as such, and should we add to these items other forms of military equipment such as guns and stocks of ammunition and so on? There is no 'right' answer to this question. It seems, however, not unreasonable to regard expenditure that results in relatively transitory benefits—and this should surely include most weapons, on which the rate of obsolescence is likely to be very high—as current—that is, as consumption or 'current expenditure' by government, even if the units produced will last for a year or two beyond the end of the accounting period. At the time of writing, expenditure on buildings and equipment for the fighting services (but not for the Civil Defence Service) is, in the United Kingdom, treated as current expenditure, though an exception is made in the case, for example, of permanent married quarters for members of the armed forces. On the other hand, expenditure on buildings and plant for the manufacture of armaments is treated as part of investment, even when owned by the government.

3. *The government account*

We now extend the system of accounts as it was developed in Chapter 2 to include government transactions. We need, therefore, a new account for government. On the receipts side we have taxes levied by central and local government, corresponding payments appearing in the accounts of firms and households. The taxes are divided into two classes in accordance with the customary distinction that is made between 'direct' and 'indirect' taxation. Direct taxes, sometimes called 'taxes on income', include income taxes and profits taxes; indirect taxes, sometimes called 'taxes on expenditure', include sales and purchase taxes and local rates.

Direct taxes are regarded as a kind of transfer to government, paid out of income by corporate business (firms account in our scheme) and by persons (households account). Indirect taxes are all recorded in firms account. The usual basis for the distinction between direct and indirect taxes is that indirect taxes are taxes imposed by reference to the level of sales of goods and services—for example, as a percentage on the wholesale price of goods sold—and the imposition of these will normally tend to raise price and reduce output. Direct taxes, on the other hand, are not related to the level of sales. There are, however, theoretical difficulties about this distinction which we cannot discuss here. For present purposes it is enough to note that the distinction is made and to indicate the types of tax which fall into each class. Similar theoretical arguments are used to distinguish subsidies, which are regarded as negative indirect taxes paid by government to firms, from transfer payments which can be regarded as negative direct taxes.[1]

On the right-hand, or payments, side of the government account we have purchases of current goods and services from firms, just as we have in the case of households, though 'consumption' now extends to expenditure on weapons of war and the like, and on civil activities of government. Then we have such transfer payments as interest on the national debt and social security payments to households, which include national insurance benefits, family allowances, scholarships, and so on: we shall include one item, called 'transfers

[1] Students wishing to pursue this further should consult a standard text, such as Mrs U. K. Hicks's *Public Finance*.

to households', in our set of accounts to represent all these. (We shall assume in the example that these are all paid directly to households; in fact national debt interest may, of course, be paid in the first instance to firms. In either case it is treated as a transfer payment, not entering into the calculation of national product.)

In our example we shall not include a separate item for subsidies. (If we like we can assume that the indirect taxation is after deduction of subsidies).

Inserting arbitrary figures, though retaining the same figure as before for gross national income, we have:

*Firms*

| | *Receipts* | | | *Payments* | |
|---|---|---|---|---|---|
| 1. (=13) | Sales of consumption goods and services to households | 85 | 6. (=11) | Purchases of factor services from households | 90 |
| 2. (=18) | Sales of current goods and services to government | 15 | 7. (See 16) | Direct taxes | 4 |
| 3. (=27) | Gross domestic investment | 10 | 8. (=17) | Indirect taxes | 13 |
| 4. (=22) | Sales of exports to non-residents | 10 | 9. (=24) | Firms' saving | 6 |
| 5. (=23) | *Less* purchases of imports from non-residents | −7 | | | |
| | | 113 | | | 113 |

Item 7 represents taxation on undistributed corporate profits

*Households*

| | *Receipts* | | | *Payments* | |
|---|---|---|---|---|---|
| 11. (=6) | Sales of factor services to firms | 90 | 13. (=1) | Purchases of consumption goods and services from firms | 85 |
| 12. (=19) | Transfer payments from government | 5 | 14. (See 16) | Direct taxes | 6 |
| | | | 15. (=25) | Households' saving | 4 |
| | | 95 | | | 95 |

Item 10 is introduced in the next chapter
Item 13 represents income tax levied on persons

*Government*

| *Receipts* | | | *Payments* | | |
|---|---|---|---|---|---|
| 16. (=7+14) | Direct taxes | 10 | 18. (=2) | Purchases of current goods and services from firms | 15 |
| 17. (=8) | Indirect taxes | 13 | 19. (=12) | Transfers to households | 5 |
| | | | 20. (=26) | Government saving | 3 |
| | | 23 | | | 23 |

*Rest of the world*

| *Receipts* | | | *Payments* | | |
|---|---|---|---|---|---|
| 21. (=28) | Net investment abroad | 3 | 22. (=4) | Purchases of exports from firms | 10 |
| | | | 23. (=5) | *Less* sales of imports to firms | −7 |
| | | 3 | | | 3 |

*Capital*

| *Receipts* | | | *Payments* | | |
|---|---|---|---|---|---|
| 24. (=9) | Firms' saving | 6 | 27. (=3) | Gross domestic investment | 10 |
| 25. (=15) | Households' saving | 4 | 28. (=21) | Net investment abroad | 3 |
| 26. (=20) | Government saving | 3 | | | |
| | | 13 | | | 13 |

It will be noted that we have made one change in the procedure of earlier chapters by showing imports as a negative item on the left-hand side of the firms (production) account. This allows the account to illustrate more clearly the allocation of gross national product under different heads of expenditure. It also allows us to derive the figure for gross national product at market prices (i.e. 113) by summing either side of the account.

Putting the accounts into matrix form, and, as before, showing investment abroad net, we have:

| Receipts by / Payments by | 1 Firms | 2 Households | 3 Government | 4 Rest of the world | 5 Capital | 6 Total |
|---|---|---|---|---|---|---|
| *a* Firms | — | 85 [1=13] | 15 [18=2] | 3 [(4=22) - (5=23)] | 10 [27=3] | 113 |
| *b* Households | 90 [6=11] | — | 5 [19=12] | — | — | 95 |
| *c* Government | 17 [7+8= (16-14) +16] | 6 [14=16-7] | — | — | — | 23 |
| *d* Rest of the world | — | — | — | — | 3 [28=21] | 3 |
| *e* Capital | 6 [9=24] | 4 [15=25] | 3 [20=26] | — | — | 13 |
| *f* Total | 113 | 95 | 23 | 3 | 13 | 247 |

Let us now revert to the basic numerical magnitudes. Previously we have defined gross national income (that is, national income plus depreciation) as the sum of payments for purchases of factor services including the undistributed profits of corporate bodies (firms' saving), profits being included gross of depreciation. In these accounts this total is given by the sum of items 6, 7 and 9 (item 7 must be included because the undistributed income of firms is taken *before* paying direct taxation—regarded as a *redistribution* of wealth —that is, as the sum of items 7 and 9). This gives us the figure of 100, and is identical with what is called gross national product *at factor cost* and gross national expenditure *at factor cost*. Why do we add the words 'at factor cost'? This has become necessary because the expenditure on final output shown in the accounts is at market prices: the sum of this exceeds the sum of factor incomes by the amount of indirect taxation minus any subsidies. This follows because we have chosen to regard indirect taxation, unlike direct taxation, as not being a factor income or paid out of factor income. Approaching the calculation from the expenditure aspect, if we sum items 13, 18, 27 and 28 that is, household and government expenditure on current goods and services, gross domestic investment and net investment abroad, we get a total of 113, as shown by row *a* of the matrix. The same figure can be obtained from firms account as the sum of items 1, 2, 3, 4 and 5. This total is called gross national expenditure *at market prices.* The differences between the two aggregates is given by indirect taxation, 13, item 8 in firms account. Which of the two aggregates is the most 'useful' is a question which can only be answered by the person making use of the statistics at any particular time. It can be said for the 'factor cost' concept that the magnitude of national product at market prices will be altered by a change in indirect taxation and this may be inconvenient if the accounts are being used to compare national products by time or regions. On the other hand, it must be remembered that changes in taxation also have secondary effects: it cannot be assumed that by using national product at factor cost for comparisons all the effects of indirect taxation will be excluded; and it certainly is not likely to be true that national product at factor cost measures the level of national product at market prices as it would have been were there no indirect taxation.

We now turn to algebra. Our original identity was

$$Y=C+S$$

which in Chapter 2 became

$$Y=C+S_f+S_h.$$

We now write $C_h$ for households' consumption and $C_g$ for current expenditure by government, so that

$$C_h+C_g=C.$$

Similarly we add a term $S_g$ for government saving, so that

$$S_f+S_h+S_g=S.$$

We then have

$$Y=C_h+C_g+S_f+S_h+S_g \tag{1}$$

or, substituting the values in our accounts, in figures

$$113=85+15+6+4+3.$$

Again, the identity

$$Y=C+I$$

became in Chapter 2

$$Y=C+I+(X-M).$$

This now becomes

$$Y=C_h+C_g+I+(X-M) \quad (2)$$

or in figures

$$113=85+15+10+3.$$

Substituting in (1) and (2) we have our savings-investment identity

$$S_f+S_h+S_g=I+(X-M)$$

or in figures

$$6+4+3=10+3.$$

Identities (1) and (2) define gross national product at market prices. For clarity it is advisable to distinguish the symbol for this concept from that of gross national product at factor cost (national income plus depreciation) by calling the first concept $Y_m$ (Y in the above identities) and the second $Y_f$. $Y_m$ we have already defined in identities (1) and (2). If we wish to derive from $Y_m$ the gross national product at factor cost we must deduct indirect taxation which we will denote by $T_i$. We then have

$$Y_f=Y_m-T_i$$

Substituting for $Y_m$ we have, from (2)

$$Y_f=C_h+C_g+I+(X-M)-T_i$$

or in figures

$$100=85+15+10+3-13.$$

Identities (1) and (2) are both ways of defining national product from the expenditure side. In (1) we chose to write gross domestic investment plus net overseas investment as

$$S_f+S_h+S_g=S.$$

In (2) we wrote the same magnitude as

$$I+(X-M).$$

We can, if we wish, write down our definitions in symbolic form from the income aspect, so that we have

$$Y_f=F+S_f+T_{df}$$

where F denotes factor incomes less undistributed income of firms and direct taxation on firms; $S_f$, at stated above, denotes firms' saving, that is, undistributed income of firms after direct tax (but without deducting depreciation) and $T_{df}$ denotes direct tax payable by firms. This identity thus repeats in algebraic form the definition given in words on page 52. Substituting the values given in our accounts we have

$$100=90+6+4.$$

To adjust this to gross national product at market prices we add indirect taxation, $T_i$, which gives

$$Y_m=F+S_f+T_{df}+T_i$$

or,

$$113=90+6+4+13.$$

4. *Further considerations*

For the sake of simplicity we have ignored some complications which must now be discussed. In the first place, when considering taxation and transfer payments we ignored what are called taxes on capital and transfers to capital accounts. A typical example of a tax on capital in the United Kingdom is estate duty, payable, in general, on the market value of property passing on death. An example of a transfer to capital acccunt is compensation for war damage paid by the government to individual persons. Although, however, it is possible to give examples of receipts and payments that fall into the category of 'capital' it is much harder to provide a clear-cut definition of these. Broadly speaking, it may be said that current transfers are those that the recipients are likely to regard as income available for normal expenditure, while capital transfers are more in the nature of lump-sum payments. The essential reason for making the distinction is that it corresponds to different types of behaviour on the part of the recipients (and perhaps of the payers). It is assumed that a greater proportion of any capital transfer received is likely to be saved than of any current transfer; and capital transfers are less likely than current transfers to be financed by cutting down current consumption. The distinction is sometimes a thin one, particularly when the payer or the recipient is the government, which is unlikely to be influenced much in its spending decisions by any single item of revenue or expenditure. Items of this kind, not regarded as 'income flows', may be recorded in the capital accounts: as a receipt in the recipient's capital account and as a payment in the payer's. In the combined capital account used in our scheme the receipt will appear on one side and the payment on the other.

A further complication is introduced by 'gifts' passing between residents and non-residents, whether persons or governments. In the United Kingdom accounts, gifts are called 'current transfers' and current transfers by government, 'grants'. International current transfers have the same final effect on national wealth as receipts and payments of income, but, though they change national wealth, they are not (in the United Kingdom accounts) regarded as part of national income or expenditure and are not passed through firms account as productive activities. When they are made by persons—a typical example is the remittance of funds by emigrants no longer ordinarily resident, to their relations at home—they are entered as receipts or payments of households and are omitted from calculations of gross national product, etc. For example, if on balance households transfer 10 to the rest of the world this amount is treated as if it were a kind of households' disinvestment abroad, saving of households being correspondingly lower. Grants are dealt with similarly in the government account.

Why are current transfers treated in this way? The answer seems to be as follows. Such receipts as income from overseas investments, it is argued, can reasonably be regarded as part of national product. The investments represent sacrifice on the part of the home country. The resources originally put into them might equally well have been put into home investment from which in due course production would have been derived. Gifts from overseas residents, and grant aid to overseas governments, on the other hand, it is argued, should not be regarded as part of the national product or income. We shall not discuss this point further beyond pointing out that it is entirely a matter of choice and definition what receipts and payments should be included in the computation of national income. (The United States national income accounts *do* record grants and remittances as part of income, positive or negative.)

Another matter which our simplified accounts neglect is the fact that in real life the government, like households, is in receipt of incomes paid in respect of factor services. The central and local governments own land and buildings and investments and have trading departments, and accordingly receive from the firms sector, just as households do, rents, interest, dividends and profits (but not, of course, wages and salaries). Hence the government account will normally record receipts of factor incomes and firms account will show a corresponding payment.

Finally, it should be noted that all government transfer payments shown in our accounts are domestic. Such payments as interest on government debt paid abroad may be, as in the United Kingdom accounts, treated in a way similar to government purchases of imports: as government payments to firms accompanied by firms' payments to non-residents.

This almost completes our schematic treatment of national income accounting. There remains for preliminary discussion in the following chapter an important analytical point: the division of the firms account into a production and an appropriation account. (A more extended discussion will appear in Chapter 9 and its Appendix where our simplified scheme is developed further along the lines followed in the official United Kingdom national income accounts.) Also in Chapter 4 we shall review some of the problems of definition and valuation which arise when we try to give our classifications and algebraic symbols a clear meaning. We shall then indicate briefly some of the practical statistical problems involved in the assignment of numerical quantities to these classifications. Finally, in Chapter 5, we shall illustrate the discussion of Part I of the book by setting out, in the form with which readers will have become familiar, national income data of the United Kingdom for the year 1965.

# 4

# NATIONAL INCOME ACCOUNTS: PROBLEMS OF CLASSIFICATION AND DEFINITION

## 1. *Introduction*

In this chapter we shall consider some of the problems of definition which arise when we try to fit into the conceptual framework of a set of national income accounts the network of interrelated transactions and value changes that occur in an actual economy. The main difficulties relate to: (*a*) the way in which we classify the economy by accounts; (*b*) questions about which activities the accounts shall cover and which they shall exclude, and the distinction between receipts and payments of 'income', and 'transfer payments'; (*c*) the principles on which the measurements are to be made. Closely connected with questions of definition are the statistical problems which arise in the process of assembling the data.

## 2. *Classification into sectors and accounts—the appropriation account*

The first problem, which has already been suggested by the earlier discussion, arises when we are considering the main heads under which we wish to classify activities. The general form of the national income accounts is derived, as we have mentioned in Chapter 1, from theoretical descriptions of the economy associated with the name of the late Lord Keynes. These theoretical models describe relationships between the main functional activities in the economy: production, consumption, investment, saving. In simple, hypothetical, examples it is possible to identify this kind of classification by function with classification by certain types of social organisation. 'Firms' carry on production, and buy factor services. 'Households' receive income from firms from the sale of factor services and use part of that income for consumption, saving the rest.

Now, if one is considering economic behaviour (and this is the idea underlying all social accounting) it may be misleading to ignore the various forms in which the transactors of the economy are organised. Company directors will behave differently from the owners of private businesses, and the decisions of both are of a different nature from those of the administrators of government trading bodies; and so on. This suggests that there may be advantages in dividing the firms, or production, account into sub-accounts, corresponding to different types of business organisation, just as in Chapter 3 we said that it may be convenient to sub-divide the government account into accounts for central and local government. Up to the present, however, no great progress has been made in this direction, probably because the necessary statistical material is lacking. If we take the United Kingdom as an example we find that the annual Blue Books on National Income and Expenditure go some way towards providing separate figures for activities of privately- and publicly-owned business corporations. This segregation of figures is not, however, extended to other types of organisation and, moreover, is only applied to what is called the *appropriation account*, the nature of which must now be explained.

The business activities of any productive organisation, or 'firm' in our terminology, can be divided into (*a*) the 'productive' activities proper, as defined in Chapter 1, and (*b*) the receipt and payment of 'transfers', so-called to distinguish them from payments arising out of the productive activities. Our firms account can be made to reflect this division by splitting it into two parts called the 'production' or 'operating' account and the 'appropriation' account. As a corollary, one of the 'payments' to factors of production in any particular operating account will be the profit for the period; and there will be a corresponding 'receipt' in the appropriation account, which will then show how much of the profit, together with any 'transfers' received, is distributed in the form of direct taxation, interest, and dividends, and how much is saved. Taking the figures of the firms' account set out in Chapter 3, it might be divided between production and appropriation accounts, as shown on the next page. We assume that the payment of 90 to households for factor services comprises employment income of 76 (debited to the production account) and interest and dividends of 14 (debited to the appropriation account).

It should be noted that the production account permits an alternative calculation of gross national income. We have already defined gross national income as the sum of factor incomes, direct taxes and

*Firms*

| *Receipts* | | | *Payments* | | |
|---|---|---|---|---|---|
| 1, 2, 3, 4. | Sales of goods and services | 120 | 6. | Purchases of factor services from households | |
| 5. | *less* purchases of imports from non-residents | 7 | 6a. | Employment income | 76 |
| | | | 6b. | Interest and dividends | 14 |
| | | | 7. | Direct taxes | 4 |
| | | | 8. | Indirect taxes | 13 |
| | | | 9. | Firms' savings | 6 |
| | | 113 | | | 113 |

*Firms Production Account*

| *Receipts* | | | *Payments* | | |
|---|---|---|---|---|---|
| 1, 2, 3, 4. | Sales of goods and services | 120 | 6a. | Employment income | 76 |
| 5. | *less* purchases of imports from non-residents | 13 | 8. | Indirect taxes | 13 |
| | | | 10. | Gross trading profits | 24 |
| | | 113 | | | 113 |

*Appropriation Account*

| | | | | | |
|---|---|---|---|---|---|
| 10. | Gross trading profits | 24 | 6. | Interest and dividends | 14 |
| | | | 7. | Direct taxes | 4 |
| | | | 9. | Firms' saving | 6 |
| | | 24 | | | 24 |

firms' saving (section 3 of Chapter 3) which equals 100. This aggregate is also necessarily equal to gross trading profits plus employment income, i.e. 21 + 79, which provides another way of calculating gross national product at factor cost from the income side. This latter approach is the one followed in the United Kingdom statistics.

A complete sub-division of the firms account in terms of types of business organisation would imply a separate production account and a separate appropriation account for each subdivision. In fact, the United Kingdom statisticians limit themselves to (*a*) a single production account, covering all types of organisation, and (*b*) a separate appropriation account for all corporate business, which is then subdivided again into accounts for privately-owned corporations (distinguishing financial companies) and for publicly-owned corporations. Thus, no separate appropriation account is provided for non-corporate private business or for non-corporate government trading bodies, and the entries which would have appeared in such appropriation accounts are, in fact, recorded in the households account or government account, as the case may be, the whole business profit being shown as a payment from the firms account to one or other of the latter accounts.

The inadequacy of the data available to the compilers of the accounts make it impossible for them to maintain perfect consistency in their scheme. For instance, because the income tax statistics do not distinguish between distributed and undistributed income of non-corporate business the statisticians have to record direct taxes on non-corporate business, and savings of non-corporate business, in the households or personal sector, though this is inconvenient, and may mislead the reader of the accounts who does not familiarise himself with the manner of their construction. There are a number of 'untidinesses' of this kind which will no doubt be gradually removed as the statistics improve and standard rules of presentation harden out. This problem need not worry us very much so long as we are careful to ascertain, when we use accounts, what basis has been adopted for the classification of activities in them.

### 3. *The transactions recorded*

National income accounts do not purport to provide a 'complete' picture of the economy, even in the limited sense in which *any* set of measurements can provide a 'complete' picture. It is not very difficult to indicate in broad terms the classes of economic events that are respectively embraced by, and excluded from, the accounts. The latter record: (*a*) the 'flow' of value arising from the production of new goods and services during the period of the accounts, classified under different heads of expenditure according to the disposal of the product (but not necessarily of the actual 'things' produced, for some of the goods manufactured during a period will go into stock, and goods brought forward from the previous period will be consumed in the current period); (*b*) the incomes accruing to the factors of production in respect of that product; (*c*) 'current' transfers of wealth, between sectors, and to and from abroad, in the form of gifts, grants, taxes, interest payments (to the extent that these are not regarded as part of factor incomes); and (*d*), to a limited extent, 'capital' transfers. (We have commented on the distinction between 'current' and 'capital' in Chapter 3.) On the other hand the accounts exclude domestic transactions in second-hand goods—that is, in goods that have left the ownership of their 'producers'—except to the extent that such goods are sold back to the production sector by consumers.

When, however, we begin to think about the nature of the goods and services whose value makes up our product, we find it difficult to draw any satisfactory formal distinction between services which are to be regarded as part of the national product and those that are not. If we are to include, as we do, the value of paid services of domestic servants and hotel workers why should we exclude, as we also do, the value of unpaid services of wives and other members of households in the home? If we include as part of the product the value of work done by professional house painters is it not reasonable to include the value of work put in by people who do their own house decoration, especially when we remember that in order to work in the home some people may sacrifice income that they could have earned in other occupations and which would have gone into the statistics? We shall not pursue these questions further here as they will be examined in Chapter 6 where an even greater difficulty than those we have mentioned will be discussed—that relating to the 'value' of leisure. Meanwhile we may note that rule of thumb decisions have to be made about what services shall be valued for the purpose of the accounts. The answer depends a good deal on the nature of the statistics available. In this country it is broadly true that the rules of assessment to income tax are followed for the purpose of deciding what activities shall be considered as 'income-producing' and brought into the calculation of the national product. In general the services that are excluded do not enter into the market and could, therefore, only be valued on an arbitrary basis. (We must remember that the converse is not true: rents are imputed, for example, to houses even when owned by their occupiers, and in the tax assessment of farm incomes an addition is made for the value of produce consumed by the household. A good deal of capital formation, too, is 'internal' to the firm.) Nevertheless, mention must be made of one class of transactions that do occur in the market and yet in respect of which no income is deemed to arise. These are the type of transaction the 'income' from which is commonly regarded as a 'windfall' or a 'capital' profit, and which is not (in the United Kingdom) subjected to income tax, even when the profit might be regarded as a factor income, as where it arises from the service which successful speculators render in improving the perfection of the market in which they operate.

Difficulties may also arise in deciding whether some expenditures should be regarded as final outlays or as purchases of inputs. For example, it is usual to treat personal expenditure on the journey to work as part of consumption expenditure paid out of the employee's income. But it would not be entirely unreasonable to regard at least part of this outlay as the purchase of an input by the employee, his income being correspondingly less. After all, if the cost of the lift which takes the employee to the office floor on which he is to work is regarded as an input (of his employer in this case) why not the cost of the rest of his journey to work? On the other hand it is not difficult to find contrary arguments: the distance to work is partly a function of the employee's choice of residence, and it is not unreasonable to regard at least the extra cost of travel incurred because he prefers a better home environment than that of the living accommodation nearest to his firm, as consumption. As always, however, the border line is arbitrary. Here, too, the income tax rules provide a rule of thumb solution: the journey is 'consumption'.

One of the conceptual problems that arises in the preparation of national income accounts relates to payments of interest and dividends. The problem here is, to what extent should payments of this kind be regarded as made in respect of current services and treated, therefore, as part of the aggregate gross national product, and to what extent should they be treated as mere transfers of income between sectors? It must be remembered that classifications for one purpose may not be those best suited for another. For example, when national income accounting methods are being used, as will be described in Chapter 7, for the purpose of national budgeting, it is not helpful to regard government payments of interest on the national debt as part of gross national product, for we are then using that concept as an index of the aggregate goods and services that can be currently produced and which, within limits, can be switched from one use to another. It is true that we can conceive of government debt interest as payment for the continuing service of providing the loans on which it is paid, but there exists no possibility of switching that service to other uses. Similarly, in making the kind of international comparison of economic welfare which will be discussed in Chapter 6, it would not be very sensible to regard a country with a very large government debt as more wealthy than one similar in all other respects but with no debt, which would be the implication of putting government debt interest in the total product. On the other hand, if we are using the accounts as a way of thinking about the complex movement of goods, services and claims in the economy and of the changes in the asset structures of various groups of people, we shall not worry so much about the national income 'aggregates', and a set of accounts designed to throw light upon the latter may be ill suited for our purpose.

We have seen that it is usual at present to regard payments of interest on government debt as 'transfers' except in so far as they are paid abroad, in which case they represent a reduction in resources available for use at home. Business payments of interest and dividends to share- and stock-holders present some difficulties. Are such payments to be regarded as part of factor income or as transfers for the purpose of the national income computation? The answer depends upon the way in which profits are treated. If the whole of profits, before deduction of interest and dividend payments, are regarded as factor income, then, to avoid double-counting, the other payments must be treated as transfers of income. If we take the other view we must regard undistributed profit as a separate factor income.

This brings us to a further problem in calculating national income or product which arises in dealing with 'financial intermediaries' such as banks, investment trusts, and the like. To the extent that these bodies receive direct payments for services in the form of commissions, etc., pay out incomes to factors of production employed (salaries, rents, etc.), and pay other firms for goods and services bought, they do not differ from other firms. In the aggregate national income accounts their receipts for services form part of the value of final output or cancel out against purchases of other firms, according as to whether they are made by consumers and non-residents on the one hand, or firms on the other; factor incomes paid out form part of total income; and purchases from other firms cancel out against the corresponding sales. The interest receipts and payments of such institutions could be treated as transfers (except to the extent that they were transactions with non-residents, which, as explained in Chapter 2, enter into the composition of the gross national product). The trouble is that these institutions commonly rely for their profit and, perhaps, for payment of part of their expenses, on an excess of interest and dividends received over interest paid. If interest receipts and payments are treated as transfers this may result in a negative figure for their gross product which in any case will certainly understate the effective payment which they receive for their services.

The simplest way, perhaps, of getting round the difficulty is to regard these institutions as receiving interest and dividends on behalf of their loan creditors and shareholders and to *impute* an expenditure for consumption, with a corresponding increase in factor income, in respect of the excess value of services over commissions, etc., actually charged: for example, in the case of an investment trust it might be assumed that the interest and dividend receipts and payments were transfers between the various sectors, but that an amount equal to the management expenses represented consumption of personal shareholders (or an input of any business shareholders). It is as if they received the full amount of the interest and dividends received by the investment trust and returned a proportion of these in payment for the services of management. Treatment in practice varies. The present practice in the United Kingdom is to treat interest and dividend payments as transfers and to make no 'imputation' for management services; 'sales' of these institutions are thus measured by the amount of any direct charges by way of commission, etc. An exception is made, however, in the case of life assurance. Here all the interest received is regarded as part of personal income of the household sector, and an imputed receipt from households is included in the firms account equal to management expenses plus profits, this being regarded as the amount of the 'sale' of life assurance services to persons. An appropriate adjustment is made in the households account.

### 4. *The principles of measurement*

The various national income aggregates are conceived in terms of exchanges at market values and even the adjustment to factor cost is based on the deduction of certain payments fixed in money terms —indirect taxes net of subsidies—from an aggregate calculated in terms of market prices. In so far as the measurements in the accounts reflect actual purchases and sales of goods and services for money, or payments fixed in terms of money, no valuation problem arises. Certain difficulties are found, however, when we come to measurements that do not reflect sales and purchases to be settled in money. The main problems arise out of such questions as the valuation of farm produce consumed by the farm household, which must be added both to income and to consumption; the imputation of rental values to owner-occupied property; and, in particular, the valuation of investment or capital formation in the forms both of fixed capital formation and stock changes, including the problem of depreciation.

As with the problem of defining productive activities, the practical statistical difficulties are to a substantial extent solved in the United Kingdom by relying on the income tax law, which includes rules for the estimation of most forms of income included in the national income accounts. So far as farm produce, imputed rent, and similar problems are concerned we shall say no more here, beyond mentioning that the imputed rents at present in use in the United Kingdom are based on tax assessments. Capital formation and depreciation, however, offer more formidable problems and we must devote some space to these.

If all capital formation were represented by the sum of actual purchases of capital equipment and stocks there would be in principle no problem in valuing the gross addition. A good deal of investment, however, is carried out by firms on their own account. Capital equipment may be manufactured and premises built by the firms that will use them, and semi-manufactured and unsold finished stocks owe much of their value to the firms which hold them. There will have been no market transaction to fix the value which should be set on these. The income tax rules require, broadly, that the valuation basis shall be 'cost', without adding any profit not realised by sale. In the case of stocks there may also be deductions for obsolescence, etc. It is important to note that although this method of valuation can give us some idea of that part of total resources annually set aside for purposes intended to bring benefits after the end of the year of account, it can give us little idea of whether the expenditure has in any sense been justified, that is, whether the returns to be expected in the future are likely to warrant the particular allocation of resources that has been made. (It should be remembered also that a good deal of the capital expenditure in any year, particularly in the United Kingdom at the present time, represents not business investment, but government outlay, on such 'social capital' as schools.)

A special problem arises in connexion with depreciation. We mentioned very briefly in Chapter 1 that in any calculation of the national product we can distinguish between a 'gross' and a 'net' addition to wealth. This distinction arises out of the fact that in the course of production, capital assets, such as plant and equipment, become worn out through use. This 'consumption of capital' is analogous to the using up of intermediate products in the course of producing final output. To arrive at a figure for the net national output or product, we have to make some allowance for depreciation. But this is not easy. There would be no problem if the capital remained unchanged in kind and quantity; then all we should have to do would be to deduct the cost of replacing the worn out assets. But in an actual economy, both the size and composition of the capital will change. As well as the replacement of worn-out capital, new asset formation will be taking place, and what is more the worn-out capital may not be replaced by identical equipment. Shifts in demand for different products and changes in techniques may result in the obsolescence of equipment. It is, in fact, not possible to give any precise meaning to the 'correct' level of depreciation, that is, to the level of depreciation which would reflect the amount of annual expenditure necessary to maintain the wealth of the community in some sense. (The difficulties here are twofold: they involve (*a*) reaching agreement on exactly what is meant by the wealth of the community, and (*b*) deciding just what level of expenditure and what kind of expenditure is necessary in order to maintain it.) Quite apart from these theoretical difficulties, variations in business practices in provision for depreciation are very great and there would be considerable difficulty in giving a clear meaning to the aggregate of all business depreciation provisions. In practice it would again be possible to fall back on income tax calculations and this has been done in the past, but these tend to be particularly unsatisfactory for this purpose, for changes in the law tend to occur fairly often and the calculations suffer from the additional defect that they are based on a valuation of capital assets at the time of purchase or manufacture, whereas for national income purposes it is the loss in value at current price levels that is relevant.

The tendency has been to meet this difficulty in what may be thought rather an Irish way—by leaving depreciation out of account and working in terms of gross investment, and gross national product, expenditure, and income, as we have done in Chapters 1 to 3. This is perhaps less of a drawback than might be imagined since for many purposes gross national product is as useful a concept as net national product. Even if we do make an estimate of the total amount that should be deducted from the gross product in order to allow for depreciation, we are still interested in the size of the aggregate from which the deduction will be made and in the component parts of that aggregate. If we wish we can assume, as a rule of thumb, that the appropriate provision for depreciation can be set at some constant percentage of the gross national product—10 per cent is a figure sometimes mentioned.[1] If one is prepared to accept this rule the gross concept becomes a perfectly acceptable one. It is merely necessary to remember that if the net figure is wanted the appropriate percentage deduction must be made. On the other hand this must not be taken to imply that the question of maintaining the

[1] Estimates of capital consumption are made for the United Kingdom and included in the annual official publication on National Income and Expenditure.

wealth of the community is unimportant. This is very far from being true, and it may be that a more detailed investigation into the problem of maintenance of the national capital than has up to now been made would be of great value.

One problem that arises in connexion with the question of depreciation is that of repairs and maintenance. When we are valuing our gross investment to what extent are we to regard outlay of this kind as adding to the value of the assets repaired, and therefore to be included in investment? On the face of it, it would seem reasonable to treat those repairs of which the benefits are likely to extend beyond the end of the current accounting period as part of gross investment. If expenditure is directed towards creating new assets in the physical sense it is regarded as investment. It seems anomalous to regard it as not being investment merely because it is directed towards existing assets, whose value is thereby raised above what it would have been. It also seems odd to regard outlay on replacing a *whole* machine as adding value and therefore forming part of gross investment, if outlay on replacing *part* of a machine is treated as without value. The fundamental conceptual difficulty is that it is not possible to impute a given addition to value, in the market sense, to any single item of expenditure: all one can do is make an estimate of the net rise or fall in the value of a given asset or group of assets and even here there is an element of vagueness. It is not, however, practicable to rely for statistical purposes on round figure estimates of value—rule of thumb procedures have to be followed, in which it is assumed that certain types of expenditure are investment and others are not. This is all the more true if the data used are based to a substantial extent on accounting records of firms in which this rule of thumb method is used.

Thus the real question is, again, what is the purpose of the account? If the object is to provide some indication of the allocation of currently available resources—that is, of additional resources becoming available as the result of productive activity—then it may well seem reasonable to include in the gross product figure all expenditure by firms intended to bring benefits over a period extending beyond the end of the accounting year, for such expenditure represents a sacrifice of resources which might have been devoted to present consumption. If, on the other hand, it is desired to obtain some approximate measure of the net addition to wealth in value terms, then the investment figure should be net of depreciation and whether a repair is classed as investment or current input does not matter so long as the depreciation figure (which will need to be smaller or larger according to the extent of the actual outlay on repairs) is adjusted accordingly.

We now have to consider the valuation of capital formation, positive or negative, arising out of changes in stocks of raw materials, work in progress, and finished goods not yet in the hands of consumers. If we are to be consistent, changes of this kind should be expressed in terms of the same price level as that for the other transactions of the year, so that the changes recorded may give a clear indication of the extent to which resources have either been diverted into stock creation or have been made available by running down the level of stocks. Similarly, if we want to have a good idea of the total national product for the year for the purpose of comparison with other years, or other regions, we need a figure for stock value changes that is comparable with the other magnitudes in the accounts. This is expressed by saying that the investment, or disinvestment, in stocks should be the value at the current price level of the physical changes in stocks. Now, owing to the conventions on which firms make up their accounts for business and income tax purposes, the stock changes recorded are, in a period when the general price level is changing, likely to diverge from the figures which would be obtained if the principle we need were in use, and the effect of these divergences finds its way into the official national income statistics in consequence of the way in which the data is collected. This can be demonstrated by taking as an example the effect of a rising price level. Most firms will calculate the value of their stock changes in such a way that the result will be a mixture of the value of the physical changes in stocks and of changes in prices. Hence, unless an adjustment is made, the figure of profit in the national accounts will be inflated by a figure representing the effect on stock values of the rise in prices; gross domestic investment and factor incomes (in this case profit) will both be inflated, and gross national product will be similarly raised. The official United Kingdom practice is to estimate the value of the physical change in stocks at the average price for the year of account in question; this gives the figure of domestic capital formation in the form of stocks. The difference between this and the total recorded change in value is called 'stock appreciation' and is deducted from the original figure of capital formation, from factor incomes and from gross national product. (The actual statistical calculations are, in fact, rather complicated and are made difficult by lack of adequate data.)

### 5. *The collection of data*

So far we have taken the figures provided for granted. How are they collected? How reliable are they? Complete answers to these questions would require a separate volume. As this is not a work on statistical estimation, we have chosen only to outline the main problems of estimation here, our object being to remind the reader that the degree of accuracy of the figures must vitally affect their usefulness. The references and the bibliography at the end of the book may help the reader who would like to consider these problems in more detail.

Now we have explained in Chapter 1 that we can look at the national income in three ways, as the sum of the net output of individual industries (national product), as the sum of factor incomes (national income) and as the sum of the purchases of final output (national expenditure). Ideally, therefore, what we require is independent calculations of each aggregate based on different sources. This would provide a check on the results, as each aggregate should be the same. Thus, in theory we might obtain national product by listing the value of goods and services produced, deducting from the total the value of those which are inputs in the productive process; national expenditure by examining records of sales of final goods and services and of capital formation inside firms; and national income by listing factor incomes derived from productive activities. In practice, independent estimates can only be made to a limited degree, partly because some components of each aggregate are only available from one source (for example changes in stock inventories of firms) and partly because of the practical difficulties in finding adequate and reliable statistics of all the items in each component.

In both the United Kingdom and the United States the statistics of national income and expenditure have in the past been largely a by-product of the administrative functions of government and of published statistical information provided for other purposes. But this has been changing in recent years with the institution of special statistical inquiries, particularly of business firms. In each country there have been three main sources of such information. The first of these is the statistics of tax assessments. In the United Kingdom the main source of information on factor income is provided from the statistics of the income tax, and, in fact, it was the original source of the earlier estimates by private investigators, such as the late Lord Stamp, Sir Arthur Bowley, and Mr Colin Clark. In the United States, on the other hand, while the Federal Income Tax Administration provides information on corporate income and that of independent proprietors, the main source of information on employment incomes is the statistics of the Social Security Administration. This is because the social security taxes paid by employed persons in the United States are related to income, and are not poll-taxes as in the United Kingdom. In consequence, detailed information of incomes of insured persons have to be kept.

The second main source is provided by the Censuses of Production and Distribution in the United Kingdom, and by the Census of Manufactures, the Census of Business and the Census of Agriculture in the United States. The Censuses provide an industrial classification of net output, including capital expenditure and stock changes, for a large part of total production. They also help in the construction of input-output tables which display the inter-industry system of transactions.

The third main source is the government accounts themselves. In each country these accounts provide information on government expenditure on final output of goods and services, both on current and capital account, and on transfer incomes and allowances. These three main sources are supplemented by many others, such as regular surveys of household expenditures and surveys of various aspects of business activities.

So much, then, for a survey of the sources of the statistics. What of their reliability? There are several obvious factors which will govern the reliability of any set of facts such as those required for our estimates. Ideally what we require is that all economic units should keep accurate accounts, suitably classified according to official definitions, and should be prepared to disclose the information. In fact, in the first place, records may not be adequate, and, in the second place, even if there is a desire to co-operate with authorities to the fullest extent, errors of computation may arise, while errors in classification are easy to make. There is one source of difficulty in the United Kingdom which illustrates the kind of problem that may arise even where it can be assumed that reporting and classificatory problems have been solved. Official statistics of tax assessment and of government income and expenditure relate to the financial year and not the calendar year. Here adjustment demands the introduction of a convention, such as the use of figures for three-quarters of one financial year combined with one quarter of the next.

On the whole, the estimates of personal income based on tax assessment are fairly reliable, although allowance has to be made for tax evasion. The same can be said of a good deal of the information included in the Census of Production. The main problem is presented by the calculation on the expenditure side. Apart from the relative lack of coverage, there are considerable difficulties both in obtaining information on changes in stocks (or business inventories, as they are called in the U.S.) and in defining the method of valuation. Moreover, as we have pointed out, we cannot make an independent estimate of stocks, because only one 'transactor' is concerned: there is no sale.

Hence, statistical discrepancies may arise in the attempt to achieve consistency in the estimation of national product from different sources. Where this occurs an assumption has to be made about the cause. In the United Kingdom in 1965, for example, a 'residual error' of £332m was shown in the accounts. (It should be noted that the size of the residual error is not a reliable index to the degree of accuracy of the figures: it is possible for large compensating errors to have a small residual.) On the other hand, errors may be detected, and data may be improved, as more information becomes available. Accordingly, it is common to find that estimates for previous years appear in revised form in successive publications of national accounts.

# 5

# NATIONAL INCOME ACCOUNTS OF THE UNITED KINGDOM

## 1. *Introduction*

We have now completed the schematic representation of the national income accounts. We have considered some of the difficulties which arise in relating the transactions of particular groups of persons and institutions with such functional classifications of economic activity as production and consumption. Here we shall, so to speak, graft flesh on to the bones of the system by presenting the actual figures for the United Kingdom.

We shall look at the United Kingdom accounts from two points of view. First, we shall set out the various accounts for the latest year available at the time of writing, 1965,[1] showing how the conceptual basis of our earlier chapters is related to the form of presentation of the official accounts. This analysis will give some idea of the relative magnitudes of the various figures in a modern industrial economy. Secondly, we shall consider very briefly the development of the United Kingdom national income over a period of years in order to illustrate some of the more important dynamic elements in national income accounting.

The system of accounting used in the official statistics is necessarily more elaborate both in arrangement and content than the one we have adopted. Even so, the structure of the official accounts is closely related to the accounts we have set out in Chapter 3 (section 3): firms, households, government, rest of world, and capital.

[1] The figures are from *National Income and Expenditure, 1966* (H.M. Stationery Office, 1966); this annual publication is often referred to as the National Income Blue Book. These and all other official United Kingdom statistics used in this book are published with the permission of the Controller of H.M. Stationery Office.

The firms account however is divided in the official statistics into a production account and an appropriation account in the way described in Chapter 4 (section 2). There is the following correspondence between the terms we have used and the title of the corresponding Blue Book accounts:

| | |
|---|---|
| Firms' production account | Gross national product |
| Appropriation account | Corporate income appropriation account |
| Households | Personal income and expenditure |
| Government | Combined public authorities |
| Rest of world | International transactions |
| Capital | Combined capital account |

2. *The national income account of the United Kingdom 1965*

These are given in the tables on the following pages, first in double-entry and then in matrix form. So far as possible, we have used the terminology of the Blue Book in order that the reader may better follow his way through the official statistics. But we have used the same item numbers as in the system of accounts set out in Chapters 3 and 4. It is therefore possible to see the relation between the formal structure described in our earlier chapters and the United Kingdom statistics.

It is necessary to introduce at this stage into our United Kingdom accounts items which have not been brought into the simplified accounts of earlier chapters; these items have been given numbers in the 100's so that they may be clearly recognised. Broadly, there are two reasons for bringing in additional items. Firstly, there are some items left out hitherto, such as government grants abroad (item 115= 120) and various payments of interest and dividends which it would be unrealistic to omit even from highly summary accounts. Secondly, for statistical and other reasons, the United Kingdom accounts for households and government contain some elements of productive activity which have not been transferred to the 'firms account'.[1] Thus, in Table 5*a*, account I, item 10 shows a total of gross trading trading profits of £5,927m but only £5,830m is accounted to the corporate income appropriation account (item 103), the remainder being covered by government trading income of £97m at item 113 in the government account IV. The new item 'residual error' shown in accounts I and VI has already been referred to at the end of Chapter 4. It represents the net statistical discrepancy between

[1] See Chapter 3, section 1.

## TABLE 5a

## NATIONAL INCOME ACCOUNTS OF THE UNITED KINGDOM FOR 1965

### (I) GROSS NATIONAL PRODUCT

*(Firms' Production Account)*

All values in £m

| | | | | | |
|---|---|---|---|---|---|
| 1. (=13) | Consumers' expenditure | 22,708 | 6a. (=11a) | Income from employment[2] | 23,468 |
| 2. (=18) | Government current expenditure on goods and services | 5,886 | 8. (=17) | Taxes on expenditure net of subsidies | 4,447 |
| 3. (=27) | Gross domestic investment[1] | 6,650 | 10. (=103+113) | Gross trading profits[3] | 5,927 |
| 4. (=22) | Exports and property income from abroad | 8,206 | 100. (=104+110+114) | Rent[4] | 1,733 |
| 5. (=23) | *less* Imports and property income paid abroad | −8,099 | 101. | Net property income from abroad[5] | 473 |
| | | | 102. (=121) | Residual error[6] | −697 |
| | Gross national expenditure at market prices | 35,351 | | Gross national income at market prices | 35,351 |

[1] Comprises fixed capital formation and value of physical increase in stocks and work in progress.

[2] Including self-employment.

[3] Comprising profits of companies and public corporations (item 103) and of other public enterprises (item 113). It excludes income from abroad, hence the need for item 101.

[4] Rent can be looked upon as a profit derived from the ownership of land and buildings; as here, it is normally shown separately in national income accounts.

[5] In the UK accounts, corresponding receipts under this head are included in the corporate appropriation account (item 106), personal sector (item 109) and government accounts (item 115).

[6] See note 2 to account VI.

### (II) CORPORATE INCOME APPROPRIATION ACCOUNT

*(Appropriation account)*

| | | | | | |
|---|---|---|---|---|---|
| 103. (see 10) | Gross trading profits | 5,830 | 6b. (=11b) | Dividends and interest | 2,176 |
| 104. (see 100) | Rent | 181 | 7. (see 16) | Taxes on income | 751 |
| | Non-trading income: | | 107. (=111) | Transfers to persons | 28 |
| 105. (=118) | from Government[1] | 252 | 9. (=24) | Saving | 3,956 |
| 106. (see 101) | from abroad[2] | 648 | | | |
| | | 6,911 | | | 6,911 |

[1] Interest.
[2] Income from abroad (net of foreign tax) less profits due abroad.

## (III) PERSONAL INCOME AND EXPENDITURE

*(Households)*

| | | | | | |
|---|---|---|---|---|---|
| 11a. (=6a) | Income from employment | 23,468 | 13. (=1) | Consumers' expenditure | 22,708 |
| 11b. (=6b) | Dividends and interest (net): from firms | 2,176 | 14. (see 1b) | Taxes on income[3] | 4,935 |
| 108. (=117) | from Government | 278 | 15. (=25) | Saving | 2,051 |
| 109. (see 101) | from abroad | 104 | | | |
| 110. (see 100) | Rent | 950 | | | |
| 111. (=107) | Transfers from firms[1] | 28 | | | |
| 112. (=119) | Transfers from abroad (net)[4] | −34 | | | |
| 12. (=19) | Current grants from government[2] | 2,724 | | | |
| | | 29,694 | | | 29,694 |

[1] Payments by firms to charities which are included in the personal sector.
[2] e.g. national insurance benefits.
[3] Includes both employers' and employees' insurance contributions; these are both regarded as a direct tax paid by employee.
[4] Funds received from migrants abroad net of corresponding payments.

### (IV) COMBINED PUBLIC AUTHORITIES[1]

*(Government)*

| | | | | | |
|---|---|---|---|---|---|
| 113. (see 10) | Gross trading profits | 97 | 18. (=2) | Current expenditure on goods and services | 5,886 |
| 114. (see 100) | Rent | 602 | 19. (=12) | Current grants to persons | 2,724 |
| 16. (=7+14) | Taxes on income | 5,686 | 117. (=108) | Debt interest, etc. (net): to persons | 278 |
| 17. (=8) | Taxes on expenditure net of subsidies | 4,447 | 118. (=105) | to firms | 252 |
| 115. (see 101) | Debt interest (net) received from abroad | −279 | 20. (=26) | Saving[3] | 1,236 |
| 116. (=120) | Current grants received from abroad[2] | −177 | | | |
| | | 10,376 | | | 10,376 |

[1] Represents the combined accounts of central and local government, excluding intra-governmental transactions. Certain government trading activities are included (hence item 113) but not those of public corporations which are included in Table II above.

[2] Represents grants *paid* abroad of £177m.

[3] Represents the combined saving of all public authorities. It differs from the budget surplus in the conventional sense. It may be convenient to list the reasons why:

(*a*) The budget is generally concerned only with the central government.
(*b*) The budget refers to the fiscal year (April–March in the United Kingdom) and not to the calendar year.
(*c*) The budget is on a cash and not an income and expenditure basis, i.e. it records only money flows and does not take account of debt changes, etc.
(*d*) In the case of the United Kingdom, the classification of current transactions in the budget is on an entirely different basis.

### (V) INTERNATIONAL TRANSACTIONS

*(Rest of world)*

| | | | | | |
|---|---|---|---|---|---|
| 21. (=28) | Net investment abroad | −104 | 22. (=4) | Exports and property income from abroad | 8,206 |
| | | | 23. (=5) | *less* Imports and property income paid abroad | −8,099 |
| | | | | Current transfers from abroad (net): | |
| | | | 119. (=112) | by persons | — 34 |
| | | | 120. (=116) | by Government | −177 |
| | | −104 | | | −104 |

### (VI) COMBINED CAPITAL ACCOUNT

*(Capital)*

| | | | | | |
|---|---|---|---|---|---|
| 24. (=9) | Corporate saving[2] | 3,956 | 27. (=3) | Gross domestic investment[3] | 6,650 |
| 25. (=15) | Personal saving[2] | 2,051 | 28. (=21) | Net investment abroad | −104 |
| 26. (=20) | Government saving | 1,236 | | | |
| 121. (=102) | Residual error[1] | −697 | | | |
| | | 6,546 | | | 6,546 |

[1] Residual error (−332) less stock appreciation (365).
[2] Before providing for additions to tax and other reserves and for depreciation and stock appreciation.
[3] Gross fixed capital formation plus value of physical increase in stocks and work in progress.

TABLE 5*b*

UNITED KINGDOM: 1965

(£m)

| Receipts by / Payments by | 1a. Firms (Production) | 1b. Firms (Appropriation) | 2. Households | 3. Government | 4. Rest of world | 5. Capital | 6. Total |
|---|---|---|---|---|---|---|---|
| 1a. Firms (Production) | | | Consumers' expenditure 22,708 | Current goods and services 5,886 | Exports *less* imports 107 | Gross domestic investment 6,650 | Gross National Expenditure at market prices 35,351 |
| 1b. Firms (Appropriation) | Profits, etc. 6,659[1] | | | Debt interest 252 | | | Corporate income 6,911 |
| 2. Households | Employment income, etc. 24,522[1] | Dividends, interest and transfers 2,204 | | Debt interest and transfers 3,002 | Transfers −34 | | Personal income 29,694 |
| 3. Government | Indirect taxes (net) etc. 4,867[1] | Taxes on income 751 | Taxes on income 4,935 | | Grants paid abroad −177 | | Government revenue 10,376 |

TABLE 5*b*—*continued*

| Receipts by / Payments by | 1a. Firms (Production) | 1b. Firms (Appropriation) | 2. Households | 3. Government | 4. Rest of world | 5. Capital | 6. Total |
|---|---|---|---|---|---|---|---|
| 4. Rest of world | | | | | | Net investment abroad −104 | Net investment abroad −104 |
| 5. Capital | Residual error[2] −697 | Saving 3,956 | Saving 2,051 | Saving 1,236 | | | Total saving 6,546 |
| 6. Total | Gross National Income at market prices 35,351 | Corporate payments[3] 6,911 | Personal expenditure[3] 29,694 | Government expenditure[3] 10,376 | Balance of payments current surplus −104 | Total investment 6,546 | 88,774 |

[1] Including rent and property income from abroad.
[2] Residual error less stock appreciation.
[3] Including saving.

estimates of national product from the expenditure and the income sides. It is conventionally included in the income account and treated as if it were a component of saving.

Our rearrangement and simplification of the published accounts has inevitably done some violence to the original statistics which we hope is justified in the interests of exposition. The reader is warned that our estimates of transfers of dividends and interest between the various sectors are particularly uncertain in cases where the Blue Book does not distinguish inter-sector transactions. But he should have little difficulty in relating the major items of Table 5*a* both to those of our earlier chapters and to those of the Blue Book tables.

### 3. *United Kingdom national income in 1965*

The main aggregates discussed in the earlier chapters can be derived from these accounts. The totals of the left- and right-hand sides of account I, and of row 1*a* and column 1*a* of the matrix, summarise the value of gross national product at market prices from the aspects, respectively, of expenditure and income.

The table below sums up the relations between the main aggregates at market prices and at factor cost. In the 1966 Blue Book, the figures are to be found in Tables 1 and 12.

| | | £m |
|---|---|---|
| Total domestic expenditure at market prices | | 35,244 |
| Exports of goods and services | 6,503 | |
| Imports of goods and services | 6,869 | |
| Balance of exports over imports | | −366 |
| Gross domestic product at market prices | | 34,878 |
| Property income received from abroad | 1,703 | |
| Property income paid abroad | 1,230 | |
| Net property income from abroad | | 473 |
| Gross national product at market prices | | 35,351 |
| *less* Indirect taxes net of subsidies | | −4,447 |
| Gross national product at factor cost | | 30,904 |
| Capital consumption | | 2,625 |
| National income | | 28,279 |

This table introduces the concept of the gross domestic product (often abbreviated to GDP). The gross domestic product can be looked at in two ways. It can either be derived from total domestic expenditure (by consumers, government and for domestic investment) by adding on goods and services sold abroad, i.e. exports, and allowing for the fact that part of these expenditures are met not by domestic production but by imports. The gross domestic product can also be looked upon as equal to gross national product without including net property income from abroad. It should be noted that exports of goods and services (£6,503m) plus property income received from abroad (£1,703m) necessarily equals item 4 of our account I 'exports and property income from abroad' (£8,206m); there is a corresponding identity for imports.

In section 4 of Chapter 4 we referred to the practical and theoretical difficulties of measuring the depreciation or consumption of capital. Approximate estimates of capital consumption are made for the United Kingdom and so it is possible to arrive at the estimate for national income shown in the table above. But, for the reasons set out in Chapter 4, it is usual in national income analysis to work with gross national product figures or, since the difference between them is usually small, with gross domestic product figures.

5. *Short-term movements in the national income*

In a later chapter we discuss the use of national income accounting to make short-term forecasts of changes in the economic situation. Any forecasting method must draw upon an analysis of the past and at this point it is convenient to note a few of the more important things to look for in a time pattern of national income statistics.

Table 5*c* sets out the main expenditure components of the United Kingdom gross domestic product for the period 1958–65. As in the table, it is often useful to group together under the head 'total final expenditure' all demands on national production both from domestic sources (i.e. consumption and home investment) and foreign sources (i.e. exports); this yields the accounting identity that gross domestic product equals total final expenditure minus imports.

An important part of any short-term analysis of an economy is the identification of the periods of economic recession and expansion or, at the extreme, of boom and slump. Fluctuations in an economy are shown up in various ways. At times of expansion, the pace of the economy advances with employment rising, unemployment falling and usually some degree of price inflation; conversely, in a recession employment may fall, unemployment rise and prices stabilise. In the national income accounting context, the essential difference between expansion and recession is this. At a time of expansion, production is growing faster than normal and this is achieved by a more intensive use of capital equipment and higher employment. And in a recession, production falls or rises more slowly than normal and unemployment rises. It follows therefore that attention must be directed to the rate of change of output.

A simple and, for our present purpose, adequate enough indication of the rate of change of output is given by the year-to-year changes in gross domestic product and these are shown in the table. It will be seen from the final row that over the period 1958–65 there was almost two cycles. The phase 1958–62 contained an expansionary period to 1961 followed by one of relative recession. After 1963, another expansionary phase started which was coming to an end in 1965.

The figures of changes in the separate components of GDP give

TABLE 5c

UNITED KINGDOM GROSS DOMESTIC PRODUCT 1958–65

*Annual values (changes compared to previous year in brackets)*

£m

| | 1958 | 1959 | 1960 | 1961 | 1962 | 1963 | 1964 | 1965 |
|---|---|---|---|---|---|---|---|---|
| Consumers' expenditure | 15,365 | 16,160 (795) | 16,963 (803) | 17,862 (899) | 18,893 (1,031) | 20,049 (1,156) | 21,380 (1,331) | 22,708 (1,328) |
| Public authorities' current expenditure on goods and services | 3,673 | 3,920 (247) | 4,164 (244) | 4,499 (335) | 4,824 (325) | 5,082 (258) | 5,377 (295) | 5,886 (509) |
| Gross domestic fixed capital formation | 3,485 | 3,736 (251) | 4,120 (384) | 4,615 (495) | 4,726 (111) | 4,898 (172) | 5,828 (930) | 6,252 (424) |
| Value of physical increase in stocks and work in progress | 105 | 176 (71) | 596 (420) | 324 (−272) | 73 (−251) | 223 (150) | 616 (393) | 398 (−218) |
| Exports of goods and services | 4,711 | 4,852 (141) | 5,148 (296) | 5,368 (220) | 5,499 (131) | 5,817 (318) | 6,110 (293) | 6,503 (393) |
| Total final expenditure (market prices) | 27,339 | 28,844 (1,505) | 30,991 (2,147) | 32,668 (1,677) | 34,015 (1,347) | 36,069 (2,054) | 39,311 (3,242) | 41,747 (2,436) |
| Imports of goods and services | 4,599 | 4,901 (302) | 5,574 (673) | 5,526 (−48) | 5,613 (87) | 5,960 (347) | 6,733 (773) | 6,869 (136) |
| Gross domestic product (market prices) | 22,740 | 23,943 (1,203) | 25,417 (1,474) | 27,142 (1,725) | 28,402 (1,260) | 30,109 (1,707) | 32,578 (2,469) | 34,878 (2,300) |

some indication of the causes of expansion at any particular time. With a simple approach such as the present one it is difficult to make any useful comment about *consumers' expenditure* since the connexions between consumers' expenditure and GDP are complex and two-way. Looking at the figures for *public authorities' current expenditure*, it is interesting to note that there is no sign that the government is varying its own expenditure to counter cyclical movements in the rest of the economy for years of small increase in government expenditure are not on the whole associated with years of large rises in GDP. The very large increase in *fixed capital formation* of £930m between 1963 and 1964 suggests that investment was an important autonomous factor in the expansionary movement at that time. The figures for *value of stock changes* show how stock-building can play an important part in the short-term development of the economy. In absolute terms, the value of stock-building is small and in most years is less than 1 per cent of GDP. But the swings in stock-building, as shown by the bracketed figures, can be substantial as compared with changes in other components of expenditure and for this reason the impact of stock-building on the economy can be very significant. It can be seen from the table that stock-building rose very much in both 1960 and 1964 at times when economic expansion was well under way. And since, for the United Kingdom, there is a strong connexion between stock-building and imports, 1960 and 1964 were also years of sharp rises in imports, and large deficits in the balance of payments.

These are some of the ways in which national accounts can be used to throw light upon short-term developments in the economy. Our discussion has been a simple one. In particular, we have not tried to disentangle the effects of price changes on the value figures and hence show what changes took place in consumption in quantity terms. This problem of the measurement of 'real' national product (i.e. national product after the abstraction of price effects) is discussed in Chapter 6.

# Part II

# Some applications of social accounting: with a further consideration of techniques

# INTRODUCTION

In Part I we have introduced the concepts of social accounting and have illustrated some of these with statistics of the United Kingdom. One use of these systems of accounts is to help us build up a general picture of an economic system as a preliminary to considering how and why it functions in the way it does. This we consider to be an important function, for it provides us with a greater insight into the interdependency of different parts of the economy. It is, however, in the field of public policy that social accounting has become an important tool, and it is perhaps in the statistical bureaux of governments and international organisations that the techniques of social accounting and their applications are most discussed and developed. In this part, therefore, we shall consider how social accounting is used by policy-makers both in the domestic and international field.

The term 'economic policy' can mean a number of things. In our context it is best considered as a complex of decisions which are intended to determine how the national product shall be allocated and distributed among different uses and what attempts shall be made to influence its size, directly or indirectly, by the various fiscal and monetary organisations of the State. The nature and degree of influence of government policy will vary over time and in different countries at any point in time as will, in consequence, the degree of intervention as measured by the magnitude of taxes and expenditure (if we consider only the fiscal system). However, whatever the complex of decisions which comprise policy, the consistency of individual decisions with one another must, except where achieved by accident, depend on a knowledge of the structure of the economy and its development. It is true that policy concerns the future and not the past. But to know where you are going and how policy will affect your path it is as well to know where you have been and where you are, and at what speed you have been travelling. Social accounting tries to throw into relief certain important features in the economic environment. The environment may change rapidly, but even to make assumptions about what changes will take place implies you know what it comprises at the moment.

As we have indicated, one of the aids sometimes considered desirable for policy of this sort is the provision of accurate information about the past development of the economy and of other economies with which relations are conducted. The question here is to be able to make relevant comparisons over time of changes in the components of the national product which may interest us, and in its total, and to make similar comparisons over given periods of time with other countries. The main problems in this connexion lie in the consistency of the definitions of the different magnitudes and in the accuracy of their estimation. The problems here are mainly statistical. We shall consider them in Chapter 6 under the headings of the measurement of real national product over time, and international comparisons of national product. We shall see, however, that such comparisons as are made with national product statistics, such as comparisons of standards of living, raise questions of philosophical as well as statistical importance about which there is a good deal of disagreement.

A second way in which many people think social accounting can be of use is in assessing what changes are likely to occur in the economy either as a consequence of, or independently of, policy. The information about the economy assembled in our accounts may thus be used as the basis of forecasting. The rationale of this use of accounts is that any government, and more particularly any Minister of Finance, has to make forecasts of some kind about future events. It is probable that these forecasts will be more efficiently conducted with the aid of accurate information rather than by intuition, however inspired. It is here than the economist comes in. In order to use the data provided by the statistician, he has not only to specify in what form the data can be most usefully arranged. He must know something about the relationships between the various transactions which take place. The ability to predict (so far as it exists) will depend on the correct appreciation of uniformities in the behaviour of national income components. If investment rises by so much, how much will income rise? What will happen if the government increases its saving next year by so much? Attempts to answer these questions are based, explicitly or implicitly, on economic laws themselves derived from observation of past events or on introspection.

This use of national accounts is still being developed. It is not established that we either possess sufficient information or theoretical knowledge in order to predict changes in the economic scene with complete confidence. However, the experience in this field provides some interesting object lessons, and methods of forecasting based on national accounts are being constantly developed. In Chapter 7 therefore we consider the technique of national budgeting based on the Keynesian type of analysis. In Chapter 8 we consider implications for national budgeting of inter-industry input-output analysis of the Leontief type which we mentioned briefly in section 4 of Chapter 1.

# 6

# THE MEASUREMENT OF THE REAL NATIONAL PRODUCT

## 1. *The problem*

We mentioned in Chapter 1 that the original interest in computation of the national product was derived from the wish to produce quantitative evidence of changes in the economic condition of the nation. Such evidence is relevant to the discussion of economic policy and to its formulation and execution by those who exercise political power. How much has the sum total of goods and services increased over the years, if at all, and how has it been divided as between different uses and as between different income groups? The answers to these questions will suggest the limits within which particular policies which affect the production and disposal of resources can be pursued.

In recent years, too, this kind of inquiry regarding movements in the national product over time has been extended to comparisons in space. For instance, a group of countries who wish to share the burden of common defence in some way considered equitable may require to know what resources are available in each country, and for this purpose international comparisons of national product are important. The problem of priorities in the distribution of capital to poorer areas may be influenced by information about the real income per head in different areas: hence the stimulus to calculations of national incomes in a large number of these areas, which has arisen in recent years. Our burden-sharing example is paralleled in the fiscal problems of federal countries. If accepted policy demands that richer states should subsidise poorer ones, then the determination of which are the rich and which are the poor demands, implicitly at least, some calculation of regional incomes.

In this chapter we are concerned with some of the difficulties, both theoretical and practical, which are encountered in providing answers to questions of this sort.

## 2. *Comparison over time*

### (*a*) *Preliminaries*

Consider the following table, which gives us the money values of the gross domestic product—that is, gross national product less net property (or investment) income from abroad[1]—at market prices, of the United Kingdom, over the period 1958–65:

TABLE *6a*[2]

| | 1958 | 1959 | 1960 | 1961 | 1962 | 1963 | 1964 | 1965 |
|---|---|---|---|---|---|---|---|---|
| Gross domestic product at market prices (£m) | 22,740 | 23,943 | 25,417 | 27,142 | 28,402 | 30,109 | 32,578 | 34,878 |

In each successive year the total rises. Can we say that this trend represents an increase in the *volume* of goods and services over the period and thus, in broad terms at least, an increase in the resources available for improvement in living standards or for investment? In order to answer this question we have to know something about price movements. A clear-cut answer could be given if we could assume that prices of all commodities had not changed at all over the period. If price is constant, and population remains unchanged, then a rising product means a rising volume of goods and services per head. Even in this example we should have to assume that the quality of all goods and services had not altered, or had improved in some definable way. Anyone with even a slender knowledge of recent economic history would not for one moment believe that these assumptions were at all realistic.

Let us now consider how we can take account of price movements and any other factors which are relevant in trying to compute national product in terms of volume, or in *real* terms, as it is called.

[1] It has become the practice to use the term 'real product' for volume measurements of *domestic* product. To avoid confusion we shall use the term 'real domestic product'.

[2] From *National Income and Expenditure 1966* (H.M. Stationery Office).

### (b) *Crude measures of real domestic product*

The oldest method of allowing for price movements in order to reduce money domestic product, that is domestic product in terms of current money values, to real domestic product, was to deflate the money values by dividing by some measure of 'changing purchasing power' such as a retail or wholesale price index.[1] In fact, this method is still used in some countries as a short-cut method. Thus, if we want to compute our domestic product in terms of constant prices, using this method, we choose a convenient base year, set our price index equal to 100 in that year, and adjust the product at current values in the other years to the base year price level by dividing by the index for each year and multiplying by 100. This gives us the product at a constant price level. If we wish, we can express the result as an index number series and call these 'index numbers of real domestic product'. If, for instance, we tabulate a retail price index from the series published by the Ministry of Labour, adjusted

TABLE 6*b*

1958=100

| | 1958 | 1959 | 1960 | 1961 | 1962 | 1963 | 1964 | 1965 |
|---|---|---|---|---|---|---|---|---|
| Gross domestic product at market prices (£m) | 22,740 | 23,943 | 25,417 | 27,142 | 28,402 | 30,109 | 32,578 | 34,878 |
| Retail price index | 100 | 101 | 102 | 105 | 110 | 112 | 115 | 121 |
| Gross domestic product at constant market prices (£m) (1958) | 22,740 | 23,820 | 25,020 | 25,850 | 25,940 | 26,950 | 28,250 | 28,870 |
| Index of real domestic product | 100 | 105 | 110 | 114 | 114 | 119 | 124 | 127 |

[1] For a full discussion of the compilation of price and other indices, the reader will find it useful to consult the companion volume in this series, *Statistics for Economists*, by Professor R. G. D. Allen.

to 1958=100, and deflate the figures in Table 6*a* by dividing by the index and multiplying by 100, we get the results shown in Table 6*b*.

Now, the domestic product can be divided into five main components: households' expenditure on consumption, current expenditure by government, investment expenditure by firms, exports, and imports, which are deducted, 'exports' and 'imports' here excluding property income. The trouble with the retail price index is that it is based on the consumption of households only. Thus we have applied to total domestic product an index of prices which relates to the expenditure of one segment of only one of the components of that product.

Search for a more satisfactory measure has resulted in considerable investigation into techniques of measuring the domestic product and national income in real terms. What follows in this section of the chapter is largely a condensation of results of this investigation.

We have already observed that we can conceive of the *ex post* national income at factor cost in three ways—as the value of the net product of the community, as the sum of factor incomes generated within a given period, or as the aggregate of expenditure on final output of goods and services net of indirect taxation. The first of these views reflects the fact that the national income at factor cost is the sum of additions to value made in all the different industries carrying on what we have chosen to regard as production. The second indicates that the same aggregate can be obtained by summing the incomes of factors of production. The third reminds us that the sum of all final expenditures under the heads of consumption, current government expenditure, domestic investment and exports less imports, less net indirect taxation, is the same figure. The more refined techniques used to give us an indication of movements in the annual production of real resources make use of figures derived either from the analysis of total product by industries and types of products, or by heads of expenditure.

### (*c*) *The net output method*

Let us assume for the moment that we have an economy with no foreign trade and no government and that we wish to measure the changes in the real domestic product by summing what are called the net outputs of the economy in each of a series of years. We shall start by considering only outputs of physical commodities.

First of all, we choose a base year, that is to say a year from which we wish the comparison to proceed. (In Table 6*b*, 1958 was the base year.) We then divide up the production sector into its different industrial sectors and compute the net output of each industry in the base year by subtracting from the value of gross output—that is, the volume of the product times its price—all the purchases from other industries—the inputs—and any indirect taxes paid (less subsidies). The sum of these net outputs will give us the gross domestic product (or net domestic product if we deduct an allowance for depreciation) at factor cost at the prices ruling in that year, or, as it is often put, at current prices. It is equal to the sum of factor incomes if we exclude net property income from abroad from these. We then have our initial statement of domestic product for the base year.

The concept of net output can be illustrated by the hypothetical case of an industry which produces a particular (homogeneous) product by the combination of labour with a single raw material. If we assume there are no indirect taxes, the value of the industry's net output at factor cost for any period can then be defined as follows:

$$n = PQ - \Pi\mu$$

where $n$ = net output
$P$ = price of product
$Q$ = quantity of product
$\Pi$ = price of raw material
$\mu$ = quantity of raw material

The kind of calculation we have just described is thus one of the ways of arriving at the value of national product, a concept with which we are already familiar from Part I. The reason why we trouble to restate the definition in terms of this simple algebraical formula is that it provides a convenient logical link with the definition of the domestic product at constant prices which will be introduced below. Moreover, this simple formula brings out the idea of aggregate domestic product as the sum of individual net outputs which reflect the value added to products by the various industries. In practice, in a given industry we should have a set of terms $PQ$ and a set of terms $\Pi\mu$, the sum of which would give the total value of the gross outputs and of the inputs of the industry.

Our next problem, once we have the base year figures, is to obtain comparable figures for other years. In essence what we want to do is to estimate the physical quantity of output in the other years. We can then compare these years with our base year and with one another by pricing these quantities at the prices ruling in the base year, so as to give 'real' product in value terms; or we can then, if we wish, express the quantity in each year as a ratio of the quantity in the base year to give an index number series. Let us assume for the moment that for each industry in the economy it is possible to measure in physical terms the net output, which consists of homogeneous goods. (This would correspond with reality if industries required only the services of factors of production, no other purchases of any kind from other industries being necessary, i.e. the term $\Pi\mu$ in the above formula would be zero and n would be equal to PQ.) Let us also assume that we know the prices of the products of industries at different times and there are no indirect taxes. If then we denote the quantity of output of an industry by Q and the price of output by P, we can illustrate the calculation of changes in the real national product at factor cost by the following table, in which the three rows represent all the industries in the economy:

| | Year 1 | | | Year 2 | | | | |
|---|---|---|---|---|---|---|---|---|
| | 1 | 2 | 3 | 4 | 5 | 6 | 7 | 8 |
| | $P_1$ | $Q_1$ | $P_1Q_1$ | $P_2$ | $Q_2$ | $P_2Q_2$ | $P_1Q_2$ | $\frac{P_1Q_2}{P_1Q_1}.100$ |
| Industry I | 10 | 100 | 1,000 | 15 | 120 | 1,800 | 1,200 | 120 |
| ,, II | 5 | 700 | 3,500 | 7 | 700 | 4,900 | 3,500 | 100 |
| ,, III | 20 | 60 | 1,200 | 25 | 55 | 1,375 | 1,100 | 91.7 |

Here we are comparing two years: $P_1$ refers to price in the first year and $P_2$ to price in the second year, and similarly with $Q_1$ and $Q_2$. Column 7 represents the recalculation, for each industry, of the value of the physical output of year 2 at the price which ruled in year 1. We then have the output for both years in terms of constant prices—in this case prices of year 1. If we divide this value in year 2 by the equivalent value in year 1 we have an index of changes in volume, as given in column 8. This index could, of course, have been reached directly by dividing $Q_2$ by $Q_1$ for each year, since

$$\frac{P_1Q_2}{P_1Q_1}.100=\frac{Q_2}{Q_1}.100.$$

In other words, if we can assign a magnitude to $Q_1$ and $Q_2$ we can obtain an index of volume change. If we also know the value of the output of the goods in question in the base year we can, by applying this index to it, obtain the value of output for the two years at constant prices. Thus, taking industry 1 in the table, the volume index in year 2 is 120. The value of net output in year 1 is 1,000. We then have the value of year 2 output at year 1 prices from the calculation

$$\frac{120}{100} \times 1{,}000 = 1{,}200.$$

This, in essence, is how real product calculations on the 'net output' method are actually made. The net output for the base year is obtained from a convenient statistical source, as described in Chapter 4. An index number is then calculated for changes in net output in terms of quantities for each year. This index is then applied to the base year net output to give the constant price net output. In practice, as we shall see, a magnitude has to be assigned to the volume index by indirect means because the quantity of gross output, which can be directly measured by counting, is attributable in part to inputs of goods and services of other industries or from abroad, whereas in this example we have assumed these inputs are zero.

As yet, all we have obtained is a measurement of the change in volume of net output for the individual industries. We do not have an index for total output. One possibility would be to take a simple average of the indices in column 8, i.e. $\frac{120+100+91.7}{3} = 103.9$. But this assumes that all industries are equally important. This is misleading and allowance must be made for the relative importance of the different goods as reflected by the value produced. The usual method is to weight the index numbers in proportion to the value of the net output of each industry in the base year. We then calculate an index for the aggregate change in net output by multiplying the individual indices as shown in column 8 by the individual weights, adding the results together, and dividing by the total of weights. In our case the relative proportions are 10 : 35 : 12 (as can be seen from column 3). Hence our index of aggregate net output is as follows

$$\frac{(10 \times 120) + (35 \times 100) + (12 \times 91.7)}{10+35+12} = 101.8.$$

We can now say that aggregate net output has risen by nearly 2 per cent over the period in question instead of nearly 4 per cent as suggested by the simple average method. This gives the same result as if we had actually repriced the output, as shown in column 7, and compared the total value, as repriced, with the total value in the base year, that is

$$\frac{\text{total of column 7}}{\text{total of column 3}}\times 100=\frac{5{,}800}{5{,}700}\times 100=101.8.$$

In this simple case the index is defined as

$$\frac{\Sigma\, P_1Q_2}{\Sigma\, P_1Q_1}.100.$$

If we use year 2 as the base year we have instead

$$\frac{\Sigma\, P_2Q_2}{\Sigma\, P_2Q_1}.100$$

which, as readers can check, gives an index of 102.2.

We now have to consider the problem of allowing for the value of inputs which have contributed to the gross product of each industry. The difficulty here is that it is not possible to give a meaning to the 'volume' of net output in a way that will allow an actual physical count to be made. Net output is a value concept—you cannot add up in any meaningful way the 'quantity' of contribution made in, say, a shoe factory, to the mixed bag of raw materials and services that are bought from other undertakings for conversion in the factory. (How much of a shoe in terms of quantity is the contribution of the worker who sewed on the sole?) Hence anyone who wants an index of net output in real terms has to fall back on a statistical abstraction.

We do not propose to discuss at any length the techiques involved in these calculations. We shall confine ourselves to pointing out, by the use of a simplified example, the kind of problem involved. Let us return to our formula for net output

$$n=PQ-\Pi\mu.$$

Now, if we can obtain actual figures or estimates for P, Q, $\pi$ and $\mu$ at various times we can calculate net output or product at current prices. Suppose that we assign magnitudes to these terms for years 1 and 2 such that

$$n_1=P_1Q_1-\Pi_1\mu_1=10\times 10-5\times 4=80$$
$$n_2=P_2Q_2-\Pi_2\mu_2=12\times 12-10\times 6=84.$$

The index number of net output of year 2 at year 1 prices is then defined as

$$\frac{P_1Q_2-\Pi_1\mu_2}{P_1Q_1-\Pi_2\mu_1}.100=\frac{10\times 12-5\times 6}{10\times 10-5\times 4}\times 100=\frac{90}{80}\times 100=112.5.$$

As in the simple case above, we shall, in general, obtain a different value for our index if, instead of taking year 1 as our base year, we take year 2, in which case we have

$$\frac{P_2Q_2-\Pi_2\mu_2}{P_2Q_1-\Pi_2\mu_1}.100=\frac{12\times12-10\times6}{12\times10-10\times4}\times100=\frac{84}{80}\times100=105.$$

This is a special case of what is known as the index number problem and arises out of the way in which the net output is defined. (The two methods will produce the same result, as the reader may check for himself, if the quantity of input of raw material bears the same ratio to the quantity of gross output in both years, or if the prices of both input and gross output change in the same proportion.) This does not, of course, mean that one or other of the two methods of calculation is 'wrong'. It merely means that we have a choice of two statistical concepts, both of which have general significance, but neither of which have any precise meaning.

We can allow for the fact that in any industrial classification there will be more than one output and more than one input by summing all the outputs and all the inputs, as shown by the following expression:

$$\frac{\Sigma P_1Q_2-\Sigma \Pi_1\mu_2}{\Sigma P_1Q_1-\Sigma \Pi_1\mu_1}.100.$$

The aggregate index can be calculated in the same way. (The form of this expression should be compared with the simple formula above for the case where $\Pi\mu$ is assumed to be zero.)

It may be noted that in practice it is commonly assumed (except where this will produce patently misleading results) that the quantities of inputs used for a given quantity of output remain constant over time—that is, that the technical relations in production do not change. This enables the arithmetic to be simplified a lot, for on this assumption it is possible to measure the change in value of net output at a given price level by merely applying to the value of that output in the base year an index of the change in quantity of the *gross* output of the industry, which, on the assumptions made, moves in proportion to the *net* output. Gross output can be found by direct measurement, for example from figures of quantities of goods produced. The expression for net output of year 2 at year 1 prices becomes:

$$n_1.\frac{Q_2}{Q_1}=80\times\frac{12}{10}=96.$$

On our figures this method shows a larger rise in the index of net output at constant prices than that obtained using either of the more complex formulae. This is because the figures we have chosen show a rise in the ratio of input to gross output in quantity terms. The assumption of fixed technical co-efficients may thus lead to some inaccuracy—even over short periods price changes can be expected to cause some substitution of inputs, while over a longer period technological conditions are likely to change.

Even the more complex form of measurement suffers from the general defects of index numbers. Over time the relative importance of different products as measured by the weights chosen will alter, new products may come into use, and others may cease to be produced. Moreover, problems arise in connexion with changes in the quality of otherwise similar products over time.

So far we have considered an economy without government, and have applied our analysis to the output of physical commodities. But a considerable part of national output as we define it takes the form of personal services; and this is particularly true of the output of the government, a large part of which is in the form of the personal services of government employees. In this case there are obvious difficulties in deciding what is meant by the volume of output. Essentially, this is a special case of the problem of quality changes. In some cases the problem is dealt with by measuring the 'output' in quantitative terms—such as the number of claims handled by a clerk in the National Insurance administration. This, however, still leaves the problem only partially solved. It assumes, for example, that a rude or unkind clerk is as 'productive' as his more pleasant colleague—perhaps more so if he handles more claims. A similar problem arises with doctors in the health service. Are three visits from a doctor who fails to cure as 'productive' as three from one who succeeds in healing? In some cases it is assumed that productivity in a given job is constant, so that product at a constant price is given by correcting total pay for changes in the wage-rate, the latter being regarded as the price of the service.

So far we have been considering a closed economy. When we introduce overseas trade little alteration has to be made in the form of our calculation of what is called the real *domestic* product, that is, the value added in the form of goods and services as the result of productive activity in the home country. The only difference will be that the inputs whose value has to be deducted in computing net output will include imported goods and services, and our real product will include value added to goods and services that will be exported.

In Table 6*c* we reproduce the results of official calculations, based on the 'net output' method, of the real domestic product of the United Kingdom for the years 1959 to 1965, in terms of 1958 prices, expressed as index numbers with the year 1958=100. In the original source from which the data was derived calculations were given under 17 industrial headings, here summarised under four main heads: agriculture, forestry and fishing; industrial production; transport and distribution; and other services, including government. This illustrates a characteristic advantage of the net output approach: a detailed analysis by industrial activity is obtained. Table 6*c* shows how an index number of 'productivity' can be made by dividing the index of real product by an index of numbers employed, taking the same base year for both.

TABLE 6*c*[1]

DOMESTIC REAL PRODUCT OF THE UNITED KINGDOM (1959–65)

Index Numbers 1958=100

| | Weights per 100 | 1959 | 1960 | 1961 | 1962 | 1963 | 1964 | 1965 |
|---|---|---|---|---|---|---|---|---|
| 1. Agriculture Forestry Fishing | 4 | 104 | 111 | 111 | 115 | 120 | 125 | 130 |
| 2. Industrial Production | 47 | 105 | 113 | 114 | 115 | 119 | 128 | 132 |
| 3. Transport and Distribution | 20 | 105 | 110 | 113 | 113 | 117 | 122 | 126 |
| 4. Other services[2] | 29 | 103 | 106 | 109 | 111 | 114 | 119 | 121 |
| 5. TOTAL REAL DOMESTIC PRODUCT | 100 | 104.5 | 110.1 | 112.1 | 113.5 | 117.3 | 124.3 | 127.7 |
| 6. NUMBERS EMPLOYED | | 101 | 102 | 104 | 104 | 104 | 106 | 107 |
| 7. OVER-ALL PRODUCTIVITY (5 : 6) | | 103 | 108 | 109 | 109 | 113 | 118 | 119 |

One of the interesting facts thrown into relief by Table 6*c* is the high proportion in value of services as compared with industrial

[1] The figures are adapted from *Statistics on Incomes, Prices, Employment and Production*, Tables A1 and G1 (Ministry of Labour, March 1967).

[2] Including government.

production in the narrower sense. Lines 3 and 4 show that the weight accorded to services in the total index (based on the 1958 value of production) was 49 out of 100 compared with 47 for industrial production of goods. It will be noticed that between 1958 and 1965 industrial production of goods in the United Kingdom, as measured by the index, rose by 32 per cent (line 2). In the same period, however, total real product rose by 28 per cent (line 5), the difference being due to the smaller rise in the real output of other services. This may be partly due to the statistical problems involved in measuring the output of services which we have already discussed.

### (*d*) *The expenditure method*

We now turn to the calculation of real product from the expenditure side, that is, the calculation in constant value terms of the various components of domestic product under the main heads of expenditure: personal consumption, current expenditure of government, domestic investment, exports less imports. The calculation may take the form of the direct measurement of quantities of goods and services comprising final output or of deflating current expenditure by means of a price index. In the former case the actual quantity of each final good or service purchased in a given year is related to the quantity of the same commodity purchased in the base year, thus providing a volume index. This, in turn, is applied to expenditure on the same commodity in the base year, thus giving the current expenditure in terms of the base year price. Where this is not practicable, the second method can be used, expenditure in the given year under each head being divided by a price index, thus giving current expenditure in terms of the base year price. Total real domestic product is obtained by aggregating the results. If this aggregate is related to the gross domestic product in the base year an index of real domestic product is obtained.

In the case of personal consumption expenditure the direct measurement of quantities purchased is often possible. The construction of indices of real expenditure on capital formation, however, involves a number of formidable practical difficulties. The problem is to collect price information for the different types of capital goods and stocks and to decide on appropriate weights. As statistics of fixed capital formation and stocks, particularly the latter, even at current prices, are difficult to compile, it is not likely to be easy to choose suitable price indices and combine them in such a way that the final result will amount to the repricing of the current year's expenditure at the base year's prices.

TABLE *6d*

(Lines 1 to 6: £m. Lines 7 to 9: 1958 = 100)

| | 1958 | 1959 | 1960 | 1961 | 1962 | 1963 | 1964 | 1965 |
|---|---|---|---|---|---|---|---|---|
| 1. Consumers' expenditure[1] | 15,365 | 16,075 | 16,724 | 17,113 | 17,463 | 18,282 | 18,970 | 19,284 |
| 2. Government current expenditure[1] | 3,673 | 3,744 | 3,824 | 3,964 | 4,091 | 4,153 | 4,228 | 4,373 |
| 3. Gross capital formation[1] | 3,590 | 3,949 | 4,728 | 4,850 | 4,576 | 4,791 | 5,909 | 5,879 |
| 4. Exports[1] | 4,711 | 4,838 | 5,108 | 5,259 | 5,344 | 5,576 | 5,783 | 6,049 |
| 5. *less* Imports and adjustment to factor cost | −7,248 | −7,817 | −8,557 | −8,550 | −8,656 | −9,067 | −9,790 | −9,836 |
| 6. Gross domestic product[2] | 20,091 | 20,789 | 21,827 | 22,636 | 22,818 | 23,735 | 25,100 | 25,749 |
| 7. Index of real domestic product (expenditure method)[2] | 100.0 | 103.5 | 108.6 | 112.7 | 113.6 | 118.1 | 124.9 | 128.2 |
| 8. Index of real domestic product[2] (see Table 6*c*; net output method) | 100.0 | 104.5 | 110.1 | 112.1 | 113.5 | 117.3 | 124.3 | 127.7 |
| 9. 'Crude' index of real domestic product (see Table 6*b*) | 100 | 105 | 110 | 114 | 114 | 119 | 124 | 127 |

[1] At 1958 market prices.

[2] At 1958 factor cost.

The problems in the case of government expenditure are not essentially different except in so far as the preponderance of services, with the accompanying problem of defining the unit of volume and allowing for quality of service which we have already discussed, raises in a specially acute form difficulties not absent under the other heads of expenditure.

As regards exports and imports, the current values are deflated in the same way as are the other expenditure items by the application of the price indices appropriate to reflect their values in terms of base year prices. The calculation of real domestic product from the expenditure aspect (which theoretically should be the same magnitude as real domestic product computed on the net output method) does not involve allowance for changes in the terms of trade or for net property income from abroad. These are only brought in if we wish to move on from real domestic product to real income.

In Table 6*d* we show the official calculation of real domestic product of the United Kingdom for the years 1958 to 1965, based on the 1958 price level.[1] The expenditure components are shown in lines 1 to 4. These are calculated from expenditures valued at market prices. Hence, in order to arrive at real gross domestic product at factor cost (line 6), it is necessary to subtract an estimate of taxes on expenditure less subsidies valued at average 1958 rates; this adjustment, together with that for imports, is made in line 5. The corresponding index number (1958=100) is shown in line 7. Line 8 shows the equivalent calculation done on the net output method, taken from Table 6*c* above and line 9 repeats the crude index as shown in Table 6*b*. It is interesting to note that there is a fairly close correspondence between the three indices though in some years the crude figure is the more divergent.

One word of warning must be given about the interpretation of figures of this sort, apart from the question of possible misleading results due to the practical problems of calculation. The figures reflect change in the economy, but they cannot by themselves explain the causes of change nor do they lend themselves to only one interpretation of these changes. A good example is to be found in the calculation of an index of over-all productivity (index of real domestic product divided by index of numbers employed). It is all too easy to assume that changes in an index of over-all productivity as shown in Table 6*c* mean changes in technical efficiency. In fact nothing can be assumed about technical progress from this table alone. Short-term fluctuations in productivity as we have measured

[1] Published in *National Income and Expenditure 1966*.

it are closely related to the course of the business cycle. Thus, the pause in the index in 1961 and 1962 probably has nothing to do with industrial efficiency, but is more likely to be a reflection of the end of a period of strong expansion partly brought about by the government's deflationary measures of 1961; in such a case, unless the number of workers employed drops, the index is bound to level off.

### 3. *International comparisons of national product*

We have already stressed that international comparisons of national economic magnitudes are not merely a matter of academic interest, but an important adjunct to official policy. For instance, the discussion of the sharing of defence burdens among North Atlantic Treaty Organisation countries has involved questions of the proportions of national income devoted to defence purposes in different countries. Measuring burdens in this way is only sensible if there exist significant and comparable data. One could argue that too much rather than too little use has been made of comparisons of this sort both officially and non-officially. This assertion can be supported by a consideration of the difficulties encountered in fulfilling the requirements of significance and comparability.

The first problem of estimation relates to the definition of national product itself. It is no easy matter to arrive at a consistent definition of the term, especially if questions of relative burdens to be borne may depend on the answer. We have already mentioned in Chapter 3 that some economists would exclude at least some purchases of national product by the government from such a comparison. Again, countries in the Soviet orbit define production in such a way that the term national product excludes the production of services altogether. Probably the main problem of those countries who more or less agree on the meaning of the term is that of non-pecuniary income, such as farmers' consumption of their own product, or the benefit of housewives' services. Here the difficulty is partly conceptual, but it is also a practical one. Any attempt to impute value to non-money income involves arbitrary assumptions.

This brings us to the second problem. It is generally not practicable to standardise procedures for estimating national product for a large number of countries which differ markedly in structure. In the United Kingdom, as we have remarked in Chapter 4, income tax statistics provide an important check on the accuracy of data derived from other sources. The value of this check depends on the comprehensiveness of earnings data collected for tax purposes. For countries like India or Nigeria, this method would not be very useful: a considerable part of the national product is not exchanged for money at all, and tax assessments are not based on careful imputations of income flows. For the same reason, estimates from the expenditure side are likely to be unreliable in such countries. These countries rely upon a net output method of calculation. Direct estimates are made of net output on the basis of production, employment and price data. In theory, at least, different methods should produce comparable results. In practice, however, the limitations of each method tend to produce considerable disparities in estimation. For example, it seems that the use of the income method tends to produce lower estimates than other methods, because of the difficulties encountered in adjusting the tax figures for evasion and exemptions from tax, while the net output method encounters the difficulty that although calculations of the gross value of production may be made with some accuracy, the deductions necessary for inputs so as to obtain net output are often exceedingly difficult to estimate. This makes comparisons between countries hazardous.

But even given agreement about the concept of national product and accurate methods of computation, there is still a third difficulty. One cannot just make estimates of product in rupees and pounds and leave it at that. One can only compare estimates by expressing them in some common standard of value, for example by converting rupees into pounds at some suitable rate, or by converting both estimates into a third currency such as dollars. The most obvious rate to choose is the foreign exchange rate existing between the two countries or between the two countries and a third country, for example the United States. The assumption behind this argument is that for the period of comparison the chosen unit of currency, say a dollar, would buy an equivalent bundle of goods in each country and that consequently any disparity between the *per capita* incomes converted into dollar terms would represent differences in the standard of living. But the use of official exchange rates in terms of dollars may be far from satisfying this assumption for they may not reflect relative price levels to any marked degree. For example, if official rates are 'pegged' any internal changes in prices will not be reflected in changes in the rate. Moreover, even if exchange rates were free to vary, there is no reason to suppose that they would reflect differences in price levels in all goods and services bought by members of the community. They would only reflect the prices of those goods which are, or could be, traded internationally.

Until comparatively recently, calculations by international bodies of comparative national incomes were commonly made in dollar terms at the official exchange rates, full recognition being given to the limitations of this method.[1] However, the development of statistics of real national product in different countries has made possible more satisfactory comparisons based on calculations of *per capita* purchasing power of bundles of commodities regarded as possessing similar utility. In recent work of the OECD, this method places the relative *per capita* income levels of European countries at least 35 per cent higher in comparison with the United States than previous estimates based on the exchange rate have done. This method, however, involves judgements of what bundle of commodities in country A is of similar utility to a given bundle in country B.[2]

In sum, therefore, the statistical difficulties which beset comparisons of this sort are formidable. Detailed comparisons of this sort have their uses in indicating probable orders of magnitude of variations in income levels, on given definitions of 'income', but no sensible social scientist will draw from them any definite conclusions about the relative economic conditions of two countries without further investigation, especially if the *per capita* income difference is relatively low.

### 4. *Real national product and economic welfare*

It will be recalled from Chapter 1 that the pioneers of national income estimation were interested in deriving a measure of economic 'progress' or economic 'welfare'. Progress and welfare to many economists were matters of changes in the production and distribution of income, and of striking a balance between the maintenance of a high rate of productivity and equity in distribution. Naturally enough, policy recommendations on such matters depend on a knowledge of both the level of production and the distribution of income over time. We are not obliged to commit ourselves to agreement with the views of particular groups of economists, because ultimately these are matters of political philosophy. But it is important for the reader to know where technical analysis ends and ethical assumptions and recommendations begin. In this final section we shall only be able to deal briefly with these matters, but at least

[1] For example, see the United Nations Statistical Papers Series E, No. 1, *National and Per Capita Incomes in Seventy Countries in 1949*.

[2] See *An International Comparison of National Products and the Purchasing Power, of Currencies* by Milton Gilbert and Irving B. Kravis (O.E.E.C., Paris, 1954). Also more recently, Beckermann and Bacon, 'International Comparisons of Income Levels: a suggested new measure', *Economic Journal*, September 1966.

we can pose the relevant questions to the reader, and leave him to consider what answers, if any, there are to them.

Let us for the moment consider the implications of a particular measure of economic progress.[1] This is the change through time of real national product per head of occupied population, in other words the movement in the total 'volume' of goods and services per head of occupied population, as measured by valuing the national product at constant prices. At first sight, all we have to do, so far as this measure is concerned, is to take the real national product at factor cost and to divide it by the total occupied population, for the relevant span of years. The accuracy of the measure, therefore, will depend on the extent to which we can adequately express changes in the volume of national product over time. We have examined some of the problems of obtaining accurate measures in terms of the index number problem, but it is relevant here to consider some further imperfections which present difficulties in accepting figures expressed in money values.

The first problem is that a very important commodity is left out of reckoning in the figures we have. This is leisure. If a given national output can be produced with shorter hours, then this ought to represent an increase in real national product, because the supply of leisure will have increased, without diminishing the supply of any other commodity. We cannot, however, conveniently include leisure in our national product and assign it a weight and a price. We have to look for other evidence such as changes in hours worked. The general point here is that we have to take account of the ease or difficulty in producing goods and services in any consideration of the magnitude of real national product.

It is obviously in matters of this sort, when we are trying to think in terms of people's material well-being, that the problem of government services is a very difficult one. A case where the difficulty is shown in striking terms is that of a war. By our usual definition of national output, a rise in the volume of current government expenditure with a corresponding fall in the production of consumption goods may leave real national product unchanged. But, as we commented in Chapter 3, it is doubtful if many persons would consider such a situation as being 'no worse' in terms of their standard of living.

These difficulties relate primarily to the definition of national

[1] This is the measure propounded by Professor J. R. Hicks in his *Social Framework* (2nd ed.), ch. 16. The reader may find it useful to examine Professor Hicks's justification of this measure.

product. The way we deal with these problems will be reflected in the numerical value of the index of welfare we choose; on the other hand, once a consistent definition is found, then the measure provided by an index number is, in principle, unequivocal, *provided we are prepared to define economic 'progress' in that way.*

Now most economists who believe that this sort of measure is significant would agree that, in the end, what they are trying to devise is an index of the well-being of the community in a particular sense. In other words, the index is to be associated with the changes in the satisfaction of the community. It is therefore not the goods bought, but the satisfaction that they yield which is important. Thus the assumption is made that an increase in real national product, by increasing the volume of goods and services, increases satisfaction in some sense or other. It is in the choice of the further assumptions necessary to establish this connexion that the frontiers of economics are reached.

Consider the situation where, for simplicity's sake, we assume a community of three individuals or households, A, B and C, whose money income is given for two successive years. We show this situation in Table 6*e*. In order to avoid our index number problem, we assume that prices have not changed for any goods, services or claims. Therefore, money income can be identified with real purchasing power.

TABLE 6*e*

INCOME

| | Year 1 | Year 2 |
|---|---|---|
| A | 400 | 800 |
| B | 200 | 200 |
| C | 300 | 200 |
| Total | 900 | 1,200 |
| *Per Capita* | 300 | 400 |

Now, the real income of A has risen, that of B has remained constant and that of C has fallen. What, then, can we say about the change in community satisfaction? Take our original measure of economic progress, the *per capita* real income. It involves a simple unweighted average of the real incomes of the three members of the community. By this method, economic progress must have taken place, because the *per capita* income has risen from 300 to 400. If we are to argue that this change also represents a rise in satisfaction, we have to argue (*a*) that individuals prefer a higher real income to a lower, (*b*) that the satisfaction of different individuals can be compared, and (*c*) that we can identify income with satisfaction. Let us consider these assumptions.

The first assumption is probably acceptable to most persons, but even this has its difficulties, because it assumes that the satisfaction an individual derives from his income is independent of the income of others. If we accept this proposition, then in a situation where the real income of *all* persons increased, or where the real income of *some* persons increased while that of others remained the same, we could say that community satisfaction or welfare had increased. But this state of affairs could include situations where the real incomes of some persons were unchanged, but where others obtained very great increases indeed. Some people might argue that such a situation need not represent an 'improvement' at all, because those whose income had remained the same might be dissatisfied with their *relative* poverty and this might outweigh the increased satisfaction of the others.

Consider now assumptions (*b*) and (*c*). Our simple example in Table 6*e* shows a situation where, while *per capita* income rises, *not all* incomes have risen. What, then, can we say of community satisfaction in a situation where some gain and others lose? We cannot say anything at all unless we can compare different persons' satisfactions. For instance, if we could say that the gain to A in a rise of 400 in income represented a greater increase in satisfaction than the decrease in satisfaction resulting from the decline of 100 in C's income, then we could say that community welfare had increased. We might, in fact, assume that units of real income were identifiable with units of 'satisfaction'. This would mean that we should be able to sum and compare different persons' satisfaction. There are many people who would defend the view that it makes sense to perform these sums, though economists who use this sort of reasoning to derive rules of public policy assume a more subtle relation between satisfaction and income. This is the well-known law of the diminishing marginal utility of income, by which the rate of increase of satisfaction as we move up the income scale is lower than the rate of increase of income. If we were using this 'law' (which is really a hypothesis) in an attempt to calculate changes in 'community satisfaction' we could not assume that the increment of satisfaction derived by A from an increase in income from 400 to 800 was greater than the decrease in satisfaction experienced by C from a reduction in income from 300 to 200. The trouble is that no one can produce a measuring rod that will provide a consistent measure of these things. If A is consulted he may well assess his gain in satisfaction at a higher figure than C's loss, and point out that a policy that will produce this change will raise community satisfaction. Unfortunately C is likely to take the opposite view. This is not to say that comparisons of this kind are useless, nor that the idea of diminishing marginal utility of income is silly because it cannot be expressed in precise terms: on the contrary politicians are making this kind of comparison from day to day, and the British income tax system has implicitly recognised the existence of the 'law' for many years. The important point is that these things are hypotheses, based on a certain view of society and are by their nature not capable of being expressed in very exact terms, though in so far as they are an implicit description of characteristics of our society they have a certain objective validity susceptible of demonstration. That is to say, we can point out that people often act *as if* one person's satisfaction can usefully be compared with another's and *as if* it is worth less effort to add a further £10 to their income than it was to add the previous £10. On the other hand, this vagueness in the measuring rod should make us cautious in drawing conclusions from the international comparison of real national incomes. It is, indeed, a sign that we are standing in the no-man's-land that separates economics from political science.

# 7

# SOCIAL ACCOUNTING AND NATIONAL BUDGETING

## 1. *Introduction*

We now turn away from the study of the past development of the economy, and its measurement, and consider its future. Can our accounting system help us to forecast future trends and, if so, how? To answer the questions of this kind fully would require a full analysis of the techniques of economic forecasting. We shall be content to give only the most general account of how forecasts are prepared, enough, it is hoped, to help the reader to understand their expression in national income accounting form.

Before considering the question in detail, it is interesting to note that the original purpose in collecting the vast quantity of data to be found in national accounts was that of dealing with the general problem of inflation in the United Kingdom and, as part of that process, aiding budget forecasts. From the compilations of national income inspired by Lord Keynes and executed by Professor J. Meade and Professor J. R. N. Stone, there emerged the annual series of statistics of national income and expenditure which were designed to throw light on the problems of war finance. In 1941 with the celebrated budget of Kingsley Wood a new technique of budgeting was manifested. The annual Financial Statement ceased to be regarded as a mere forecast of the financial account of the government and became the annual blueprint for a mechanism designed to preserve the balance of the economy, with particular reference to the war-time problems of inflation. The structure of the budget for the financial year was closely linked with the calculations of the expected national income and the official decisions regarding its disposal.

It must be remembered, however, that during the war period the implementation of the budget was not by any means the only method by which the government exercised control over the use of resources. In fact, the budget was overshadowed by 'direct' controls of all sorts, from control of manpower to the control of all vital raw materials. But the theory and practice of national budgeting were developed during this period, and both administrators and politicians, as well as academic economists, became familiar with the techniques involved. Similar developments took place in the United States somewhat later in the war.

Over the last twenty years or so, the technique of national budgeting has developed enormously and has been applied in a vast range of countries both high-income and low-income. The preoccupation with economic stability, and particularly the problems of inflation, has meant that the original purpose of the technique is still of direct relevance to economic policy. Obviously, to fulfil this purpose, emphasis is placed on short-term forecasting. We shall consider the place of national accounts in this policy context in the next two sections of this chapter. In both high-income and low-income countries, however, the desire to improve living standards, if possible at a more rapid rate than in former times, has led to the preparation not only of annual but multi-annual national budgets usually covering a period of five years. This policy objective and its quantitative expression are not considered here, but it can be assumed that the social accounting presentation is very similar to that found in short-term analysis.

## 2. *The theory of short-run national budgeting*

Let us consider an economy in which there are the following primary aims of government economic policy:

(*a*) the maintenance of full employment without inflation;

(*b*) the maintenance of a given level of government expenditure, and

(*c*) the prevention of balance of payments deficits.

Let us assume that these aims were realised for a particular year. If we had the national income accounts of that year we should be able to show the relation between these objectives and the values of the main national expenditure components. As we know from Part I, Chapter 3:

gross national product at market prices ($Y_m$) = households' consumption ($C_h$) + government current expenditure ($C_g$) + gross domestic investment (I) + exports − imports (X − M).

Aim (a) could, with given wage and price levels, be expressed in terms of a stated numerical value of $Y_m$; aim (b) could be stated in terms of a minimum level of $C_g$; and aim (c) could be expressed by saying that X–M must not be less than zero. Now, our accounts would tell us what the actual values of the different components were, but they would tell us nothing about the *process* which had brought about the numerical values shown in them. To obtain, as is necessary for planning purposes, a picture of this process, we need some theory regarding the relationships between the various components. We shall try to explain how Keynesian analysis can help with this problem. The reader is warned that the model we shall choose only considers *some* of the relationships and is relevant for a much simpler economy, even, than we have chosen to describe in Chapter 3. However, it will give us some idea of what is implied by the condition that the aims of government policy should be consistent with one another.[1] The reader must also remember that not everyone would agree that the forms of intervention here assumed to be used to make these aims consistent are the only, or even the best, ones, or, indeed, that the aims themselves are acceptable. We discuss these aims and methods of their attainment because they are relevant to contemporary policy.

Let us now put ourselves in the place of the government considering, at the beginning of a given year, what fiscal policy is likely to be consistent with the policy aims we have outlined above. We must now consider how the levels of the various components of gross national product are related. We begin by assuming that the values of certain components are *given*, that is to say that they will not vary with movements in the other components. This is a not wholly unacceptable assumption so far as government expenditure is concerned, but

[1] Our model has been made particularly simple because our aim here is to illustrate the nature of the reasoning that will be used and not to discuss the relative merits of different theories. The student who wishes for guidance on these should consult such a standard economic text as R. G. Lipsey, *An Introduction to Positive Economics* (2nd ed., 1966). Nevertheless, it is as well to point out that it is doubtful whether even the most complicated theory can do more than provide a framework for thought about these problems by showing the kind of relationships which may be important. Certainly no theory yet exists which can be used for accurate and reliable prediction. Anyone who had such a theory could at once make his fortune on the stock market and retire—provided he kept his knowledge to himself!

involves a serious over-simplification if we apply it to investment and exports as we shall. However, as a first approximation it is convenient to consider these as given, or 'autonomous', to use economists' jargon. We represent these assumptions by using a symbol with a bar over it for the fixed terms, so that

$$Y_m = C_h + \overline{C}_g + \overline{I} + \overline{X} - M \qquad (1)$$

We have now to consider consumption of households and imports. Let us suppose that consumption expenditure of households is a fixed proportion of personal income after direct taxation, the latter being assumed to be a proportional income tax. We shall also suppose that imports are a fixed proportion of households' consumption. In order to simplify our procedure we shall also suppose that there are no business profits, i.e. $S_f$, $T_i$, $T_{df}$ of Chapter 3 are all zero. Accordingly, as we can see from p. 54, factor income paid to households (F) is equal to gross national income at factor cost ($Y_f$). Calling the ratio of consumption to income c, and the income tax rate t, we can express the relation between consumption and gross national income at factor cost as follows:

$$C_h = c(Y_f - tY_f) = cY_f\,(1-t) \qquad (2)$$

and writing m for the proportion of personal consumption represented by imports we have from (2)

$$M = mC_h = mcY_f\,(1-t) \qquad (3)$$

Now taking (1) and substituting from (2) and (3) we have

$$Y_f = C_h + \overline{C}_g + \overline{I} + \overline{X} - M$$

whence

$$Y_f = cY_f\,(1-t) + \overline{C}_g + \overline{I} + \overline{X} - mcY_f\,(1-t)$$

$$= \frac{\overline{C}_g + \overline{I} + \overline{X}}{1 - c(1-m)\,(1-t)} \qquad (4)$$

Now, suppose we can assume that in the year to come the maximum level of gross national income at factor cost *at existing prices* is 100, that $\overline{C}_g$ will be 25, $\overline{I}$ will be 15, $\overline{X}$ will be 20, c will be $\frac{4}{5}$ and m will be $\frac{1}{3}$, leaving t unknown. By substituting these values in our equation, we find that a proportional tax rate of 25 per cent (i.e. $t = \frac{1}{4}$) would satisfy the equation, that is to say would satisfy the condition that national income at factor cost must be equal to national expenditure at factor cost. In other words, the tax rate consistent with full employment without a price level rise is 25 per cent. We can check this by substituting in identity (1) the values obtained for $C_h$ and M together with the known constants, thus

$$Y_f(100) = C(60) + \bar{I}(15) + \bar{C}_g(25) + \bar{X}(20) - M(20).$$

It will be noted that there is no surplus or deficit on the balance of payments (for $\bar{X} - M = 0$)—the figures have been deliberately chosen to make it so—and that all the values are consistent with a full employment level of income ($Y_f = 100$).

Now consider what will happen if $\bar{C}_g$ will be higher by 6, i.e. 31 instead of 25, perhaps because of an intended increase in social expenditure. With no change in the values of $\bar{I}$, $\bar{X}$, c, m, or t, $Y_f$ will now be 110 as can be calculated by substituting in (4). However, we have already defined the maximum level of gross income, $Y_f$, at existing prices, to be 100. Thus the higher level of *money* income—income in terms of current values—following the increased government demand for current goods and services will not be accompanied by a proportionate increase in the *volume* of goods and services produced. In consequence, there will be a rise in the general price level which will by inconsistent with objective (*a*) on p. 114. Moreover, with a higher increase in money income there will be an increase in imports. Substituting in equation (3) we find that imports will rise to 22. As exports will, by definition, remain at the previous level, 20, there will be a deficit on the balance of payments, and thus objective (c) will not be realised. Given our assumptions, the only way in which a rise in prices could be counteracted and an adverse balance of payments avoided would be a rise in general productivity and/or an improvement in the terms of trade sufficient to offset in real terms the rise in aggregate demand produced by the increased government expenditure.

Given that the three aims are still in force, the government will thus have to find some method of counteracting the effects produced by the rise in its own expenditure. If it confines its action to the use of fiscal policy, that is to say, to the alteration of the magnitudes of the various components of the government account, then in our simplified economy it would either have to lower the level of other government expenditure so that the total of $\bar{C}_g$ remained at its previous level, or it would have to alter the value of t, that is to say raise the tax rate; or use a combination of both methods. In our example, $Y_f$ could be maintained at 100, that is to say at the 'full employment' level, given no productivity changes, if the tax rate were raised from $\frac{1}{4}$ to $\frac{29}{80}$,[1] while imports would then (from equation (3) ) be 27, giving a favourable balance of payments of 3, i.e. $20-17$.[2]

It would be wrong, however, to give the reader the impression that the preparation of fiscal policy is simply a matter of adjusting tax rates and expenditures. Quite apart from the political problem of the acceptability of a given policy, there is the whole question of the possibility of being able to determine with accuracy the values of the various components of national income. This is the task of the statisticians and economists employed by the government. They are not responsible for the execution of policy but for the provision of the analysis which will tell the policy-maker what sort of economic conditions will be relevant to his decisions. Let us consider the task of these specialists in a little more detail.

The first point which will have to be considered is whether or not all the relevant factors governing the formation of national income are taken into account in the theory—whether, that is, our equations are adequate. We know already, for instance, that even in our very simple model, business saving, direct taxes on business and indirect taxes have been left out of account, and we have assumed that the levels of investment and exports are given. There are many other important gaps. There are also more fundamental limitations in the type of theory we have described, for it is inadequate to portray the continuous process of change: it is not 'dynamic'. (New and improved types of theory are now being developed. We cannot, however, discuss these here.)[3]

The second point which will concern our specialists is whether it is possible to assign values to the various components of equation (4) on p. 116, even assuming that the form of the equation is acceptable. Consider the case mentioned above where it was assumed that government policy demanded a rise in government expenditure. Any knowledge of the final effect of this change would require (i) the prediction of the level of exports, investment, government expendi-

[1] We arrive at this figure by substitution in equation 4. As t is the only unknown, then

$$100=\frac{31+15+20}{1-\frac{4}{5}((1-\frac{1}{3})\,(1-t))}$$

whence

$$t=\frac{29}{80}$$

[2] One of the simplifications implicit in this model is that the import content of additional government expenditure is zero. Hence, if personal expenditure is reduced in step with the increase in government expenditure the balance of payments will not only be maintained: it will be improved.

[3] For example, theories examining the 'wage-price spiral' which has no place in our model.

ture; (ii) the prediction of the values of *m* and *c*, and (iii) the prediction of changes in productivity and the terms of trade which might shift the full employment level of $Y_f$. These matters concern the econometrist—the economist who attempts to assign orders of magnitude to our various symbols. He will need to have at his disposal detailed information of the past values of the various components of national income and any other related data. Even then, whatever he is able to tell us about the values of the various symbols in the past, there is still the problem of determining whether these values will hold for the future.

Finally, our model illustrates another difficulty facing the specialist who is concerned with either the economic or econometric problem. Our model does not give us a complete forecast over a determinable period. It merely tells us what the initial level of national income will be, on certain assumptions, and what the new level will be, given the change in government expenditure. But this adjustment from one level of income to another must take time, so that throughout the whole period of adjustment we have to assume that the relation between the various aggregates, for instance between consumption expenditure and the level of national income, will remain stable. Take the case of the government. We have no reason to suppose that the planning period of the government, often the fiscal year, is identical with the length of time of this adjustment. Objectives of policy and thus the values of the components controlled by the government may change before the period of adjustment is completed.

We must now consider how our specialists tackle these problems of estimation.

### 3. *The practice of short-run forecasting in the United Kingdom*

From 1947 until 1951 it was the official practice to publish short-term forecasts[1] expressed in the national income accounting form, but these were discontinued, it seems, partly because of the large margins of error which are inevitable in forecasts for an economy as 'open' as the United Kingdom, and partly because the forecasts might lead to speculations about government intentions which might alter the data upon which the forecasts were based. Other developed countries are less cautious, but in all cases great care is taken to emphasise that estimates of future components of the national income and its components are based on 'conditional hypotheses'—'if this happens, then this will follow'—and to reveal only in very

[1] See, for example, *Economic Survey for 1951* (HMSO, February, 1951).

general terms what policies are implied by the forecasts. Short-term forecasts are still carried out by the Treasury with the help of other Government Departments and estimating procedures have been published, but to obtain a detailed published forecast we have to rely upon outside bodies, such as the National Institute of Social and Economic Research. It can be assumed that the forecasting procedures of both the Treasury and NIESR are very similar and that the example we have taken from the NIESR *Economic Review* corresponds fairly closely with official procedures.

The first step in any forecast is to review recent trends in the economy as manifested in national income magnitudes, following the principle that it is as well to find out where one has come from and where one is before reviewing in what direction one may travel. This sounds a relatively straightforward matter of statistical collection, but in practice forecasts for a calendar year, in our example, 1966, even if prepared within that year itself, may have to be begun without an accurate picture of the past year. In recent times, however, the preparation of estimates of past movements of national income components on a quarterly basis has produced a substantial improvement in knowledge of the 'point of departure'.

As we have seen, the general question being asked of a forecast is whether or not total aggregate demand will balance total output available to satisfy it over a given period of time at some given set of prices. This immediately suggests the next step—the forecast should begin with an analysis of the components of aggregate demand. Our model suggests one way of doing this, namely to make direct estimates of the components of the 'multiplicand' in equation (4), estimate the import and consumption coefficients, $c$ and $m$, assume some tax coefficient, t, and then solve the equation. Actual practice is not quite like this. First of all, it has to reckon with a much more complex economic situation than that described in the model—more variables and more parameters. Secondly, our model assumes that we begin from one equilibrium situation and proceed to another. It cannot be assumed that, say, end-1965 saw the economy in equilibrium and that the estimated changes in the variables and parameters will produce a new equilibrium level in national expenditure neatly within the forecasting period. Thirdly, while the model before the forecasters is a good deal more complicated than the one described, the examination of the causal relationships postulated in the model is a good deal cruder than that suggested at the beginning of the paragraph. While attention is paid to econometric investigations which may throw light on the effects of one variable on another, the official methods employed, and those of the NIESR, can be described as one in which 'the components of demand are built up, largely by a process of successive approximation, into a total which is internally consistent on the basis of past experience'.[1]

Accordingly, all the components of national expenditure other than personal consumption are treated as independent variables, more or less. The value of *Public Authorities' consumption* is based on budget estimates for central government and that of local governments on the general and specific grants paid to them by the central Exchequer. *Fixed Investment* is calculated from intentions and plans by both the private and public sector culled from a variety of sources. *Investment in Stocks* is a rather troublesome item to forecast, and estimates rely much more on economic analysis of past trends which suggest a cyclical fluctuation in the ratio of stocks to total output which can be extrapolated, taking account of conditions in the different production sectors of the economy. The value of *Exports* is based on estimates of sales to different areas using surveys of overseas markets which themselves have to process a whole host of factors such as competition from other countries, trade policies abroad and so on.

When we turn to the estimates of *personal consumption*, we can easily see why the method of 'successive approximations' is an attempt to resolve an important difficulty. In fact, personal consumption will ultimately depend very largely on the incomes received from the sale of output, but these sales themselves will depend upon aggregate demand or expenditure of which personal consumption is a major component! The way out of this difficulty is to look at past trends and to have a cockshy at personal consumption forecast which would be roughly in line with the forecasts already made of the other components of national expenditure. This forecast can then be modified in the light of estimated changes in national output if these output estimates suggest a level of personal income which is not in line with the original estimates of personal consumption. Similarly, *imports*, while they may be directly estimated by extrapolating past trends, have to be reconciled with output and personal consumption forecasts, depending (as they must) on trends in these important aggregates.

Once the aggregate demand (national expenditure) estimates are made, the next step is to find out whether its aggregate level at some given set of prices will employ all the resources available to satisfy

[1] See 'The United Kingdom: Short-Term Economic Forecasting' in *Techniques of Economic Forecasting*, OECD, Paris, 1965, p. 130.

it or whether it will call for more resources or leave resources under-utilised. The prospects for output changes depend upon a host of technical factors but, broadly speaking, what the forecasters are after is a review of the changes in labour inputs, which will depend upon the size and distribution of the working population and the number of hours worked, and the changes in the productivity of labour which will depend in turn on the expected changes in the size and composition of the stock of plant and equipment. There is a noticeable official reticence about the calculation of changes in potential output which is understandable once one probes into the difficulties of constructing an aggregate 'production function' for the economy. We need only concern ourselves with the results of such calculations as recorded in our accounting schema rather than with the methods.

In Table 7 we reproduce a summary of the forecasts made for two single years, 1965 and 1966, by the NIESR crystal-gazers drawn up in the form of a 'balance of resources' table. The methods of forecasting used are substantially those just described, but the tables themselves require some elucidation and the reader is urged to compare our remarks below with those found in the articles from which the table has been compiled.[1]

(*a*) In preparing the forecast, the NIESR show output and expenditure in balance. What this balance means is that this is what the national income accounts are expected to look like, given the price changes which will bring demand into line with supply *and with no change in existing government policies.* For example, having presented the 1966 forecast, the authors explain that its implications have very little likelihood of spare capacity, and thus continuing high employment, some slight rise in retail prices and a continuing balance of payments of deficit. Any change in existing government policies, they hold, has to concentrate, as in the previous year, on improving the balance of payments and they suggest a number of alternative remedies.

(*b*) The Table shows very clearly the difficulties encountered in forecasting when the immediate estimate for the past are provisional only. Thus what looks like a remarkably accurate global forecast for 1965 (but cf. note (c) below) when compared with the February 1966 estimate of the actual figure for GDP, does not look quite so skilful when later, and presumably more accurate, estimates of the actual figure are known. It is a moot point whether or not this result is in-

[1] See *National Institute Economic Review*, no. 31, February, 1965, pp. 4–13; no. 35, February, 1966, pp. 4–12; and no. 39, February, 1967, pp. 4–13.

evitable; because it is reasonable to suppose that provisional estimates of the actual total GDP for a past year may themselves have to be based on the forecast adjusted to take account of any changes in government policy as a result of budgetary and other measures.

(*c*) At first sight, one might be led to conclude that the forecasters did rather better in predicting for 1965 than 1966 (cf. row 7 of Table 7). Such a conclusion would indicate a lack of appreciation of the technique of national budgeting. As explained in (*a*) above, the

TABLE 7

COMPARISON OF FORECASTED AND ACTUAL CHANGES IN GROSS DOMESTIC PRODUCT AND ITS COMPONENTS (£M)

| | 1965 | | | 1966 | |
|---|---|---|---|---|---|
| | Forecast | Actual February 1966 estimate | Actual February 1967 estimate | Forecast | Actual February 1967 estimate |
| 1. Consumption | 19,319 | 19,256 | 19,284 | 19,636 | 19,588 |
| 2. Investment | | | | | |
| a. Fixed investment | 5,708 | 5,528 | 5,520 | 5,648 | 5,544 |
| b. Changes in stocks | 305 | 360 | 360 | 260 | 252 |
| 3. Government expenditure | 4,370 | 4,420 | 4,360 | 4,760 | 4,500 |
| 4. Exports | 5,915 | 5,964 | 6,048 | 6,396 | 6,244 |
| *minus* 5. Imports | −6,296 | −6,304 | −6,353 | −6,460 | −6,516 |
| *minus* 6. Adjustments to factor cost | −3,656 | −3,556 | −3,484 | −3,636 | −3,568 |
| 7. Gross Domestic Product at factor cost | 25,666 | 25,668 | 25,736 | 26,604 | 26,008 |

Source: *National Institute Economic Review*, loc. cit.

Note: Adjustments to factor cost consist mainly in the removal of the indirect taxes (less subsidies) component of the national accounts.

forecast is based on the assumption that there are no changes in government policies. The forecasters cannot be expected to be held responsible for the changes that are introduced, and therefore for not predicting accurately the value of those components, e.g. government expenditure, which depend on those changes. It could be further argued that if the purpose of the forecast by the NIESR is to influence government policy then to the extent that they are successful in doing so, they automatically falsify their own predictions! It follows that in measuring the success or otherwise of a prediction, either we have to ask the pundits to make a forecast, which predicts government behaviour as well as that of other decision-makers, and which can be compared *ex post* with actual results. Alternatively, we have to compare the existing forecasts with some hypothetical magnitude and its components which assumes that government policies have not changed over the relevant period.

4. *Concluding remarks*

When the first edition of this work appeared, it was felt necessary to defend the practice of national budgeting at some length, largely because of common misunderstandings which had arisen concerning its techniques and application. Indeed, four years after the book first appeared in 1954, an official West German report on social accounting argued that its use for prediction purposes implied an acceptance of a socialist ideology. Today, as already explained, national budgeting is extensively used in developed countries (including West Germany), but, although its official employment is a function of growing acceptance of economic planning, the considerable differences in the priorities assigned to the various economic objectives, and in the choice of techniques, makes it clear that forecasting national income magnitudes is not eschewed by those who would place firm limits on government intervention.

Sufficient has been said to indicate that forecasting techniques which produce statistical estimates within a social accounting framework must undergo considerable improvement if they are to offer an accurate guide to policy-makers. It might be contended that the inherent difficulties of prediction in economics are so great that enthusiasts for econometrics are perhaps over-optimistic about the pace of technical progress in their special field. However, an assessment of the scientific aspirations of statistical estimation of national income magnitudes is beyond the scope of an introductory work.

# 8

# THE INPUT-OUTPUT TABLE

## 1. *Introduction*

As we have remarked in the previous chapter, if it is granted that it is useful to try to forecast the direction of movement of the economy, then it is clear that improvements in both the theoretical apparatus and the co-related empirical data are needed. The Keynesian type of model, while it has considerable interpretative value, is too simplified, particularly for long-term projections. It assumes that national output is a homogeneous entity, and does not allow us to trace the consequences of changes in any particular part of the production sector. Here we shall indicate to the reader an elaboration of the Keynesian system that has been developed. This is the so-called Leontief input-output analysis, to which we introduced the reader very briefly in Chapter 1.

## 2. *The input-output table*

Let us return to our example in section 4 of Chapter 1. There we showed that it is possible to break down the production sector of the economy into as many parts as is considered convenient. As soon as we split up the production sector into industrial sub-sectors, we introduce further flows between the different industries themselves. Agriculture may purchase from industry 'inputs' such as fertilisers, as well as purchasing the direct services of labourers; and industry in turn may purchase, as 'inputs', agricultural products for processing, as well as the direct services of wage-earners. For each industrial sector also, output will be sold, not only to 'final buyers' outside the production sector, but to other firms within it.[1] Now it is true that in order to calculate the gross national product, inter-industrial transactions of this sort are not included, because this would involve double-counting. We should be counting 'inputs' both when purchased at the intermediate stage and when embodied in final goods and services.

However, this must not lead us to forget the fact that the industrial origin of the national product depends upon this complicated inter-relationship between industries.

In order to examine this inter-relationship we have to know something about the actual purchases and sales of the different sub-sectors within the production sector. We also need a theory about the relation between changes in these purchases and sales.

Let us begin with the first of these matters. We can relate the type of matrix introduced in Chapter 1 to the actual data of inter-industry transactions for the United Kingdom, following the method of presentation first adopted by Wassily Leontief in his *The Structure of American Economy (1919–29)* and subsequently developed by him and other writers. The Central Statistical Office provides information of this kind in a table in the Blue Book on *National Income and Expenditure 1966* which distinguishes 14 sub-sectors of the production sector as follows:

(1) Agriculture, forestry and fishing
(2) Coal mining
(3) Other mining and quarrying
(4) Food, drink and tobacco
(5) Mineral oil refining
(6) Other chemicals and allied industries
(7) Metal manufacture
(8) Engineering and allied industries
(9) Textiles, leather and clothing
(10) Other manufacturing
(11) Construction
(12) Gas, electricity and water
(13) Services (transport, distributive trades, banking etc.)
(14) Public administration (defence, public health etc.)

[1] 'Purchases by final buyers' include expenditure on investment. This raises certain conceptual difficulties. The point is that investment is really an input of the production sector, but one that is spread over more than one accounting period. It is only undertaken in order that output may be yielded at a later date. Much output that in a twenty-year accounting period would be wholly used up and therefore not classed as part of final output at all, is, in a one-year period, more conveniently classified in this way. The important thing, as always, when interpreting statistics is to be clear on what basis they have been prepared.

In order to simplify our exposition, we have reduced these sub-sectors to only two, a manufacturing sector comprising sub-sectors (4) to (10) and a residual non-manufacturing sector. Ideally it would be desirable to show our matrix as a precise development of the matrix given in Chapter 5 for the British economy in 1965, so that the only alteration in the latter would be a sub-classification of the production row and column. However, the latest year for which we have an official input-output table is 1963, and there is the further difficulty that our previous presentation is not entirely suitable for this purpose.

In order to understand the modifications introduced in the presentation of the table, the reader is referred to Table 8*a* below. Corresponding to the production row and column in our matrix presentation in Chapter 5, we now have rows and columns (1) to (2) showing the industrial breakdown into two main sub-sectors with the inter-industry transactions explicitly laid out. So far as the payments are concerned, we require no modification in our previous scheme, except that the payments to each sub-sector of the production sector from non-residents, government, households and 'capital' are explicitly given. However, there are some modifications on the receipts side. Thus, instead of showing imports as negative exports, so as to derive gross national product by summing the receipts of the production row, some imports are shown explicitly as firms' inputs, and payments for imports by other sectors are shown separately. Again, the Central Statistical Office has chosen to deal with indirect taxes in a different way. Taxes paid by manufacturers are shown as such, but taxes imposed on goods not processed in the country, such as import duties, and purchase taxes levied at the wholesale stage of production, are treated as if they were paid not by firms, but by the final buyer. Finally, the incomes received by households and by the government from firms, together with business saving before direct taxation, are all shown together (row 5). It must also be pointed out that not all the transactions normally put in the income accounts are to be found in this table. Thus transfers from government to households do not appear and net property income received from abroad is not recorded.

The omission of this last item makes it impossible to derive the gross national product from this table. However, the gross domestic product at market prices (£30,109m) can be derived in two ways. On the one hand, it can be obtained by summing total expenditure at market prices by final buyers (equal to £36,069m in row 6, column 7) and subtracting from it imports of goods and services (£5,960m).

Or it can be obtained direct from the total of 'Incomes and depreciation' (i.e. total factor incomes before providing for depreciation, equal to £26,637m) to which should be added indirect taxes less subsidies (£3,472m). GDP at factor cost (£26,637m) also can readily be derived. The reader will find it instructive to compare the derivation of gross domestic product from the input-output table with the 1963 figures of Table 5*c* showing the expenditure components of GDP.

It is important to note that the degree of aggregation of industrial sectors in an input-output table affects the numerical measures of

TABLE 8*a*

INPUT-OUTPUT TABLE FOR UNITED KINGDOM, 1963[1]

(£m)

| | *Intermediate Purchases by* | | *Purchases by final buyers* | | | | | |
|---|---|---|---|---|---|---|---|---|
| Sales by | (1) Manufacturing | (2) Non-Manufacturing | (3) Households | (4) Government | (5) Capital | (6) Exports | (7) Total | (8) Total out-put |
| (1) Manufacturing | — | 3,679 | 6,548 | 1,097 | 2,015 | 3,794 | 13,454 | 17,133 |
| (2) Non-manufacturing | 4,119 | — | 10,441 | 3,770 | 2,699 | 1,847 | 18,757 | 22,876 |
| (3) Imports | 2,527 | 1,112 | 1,689 | 163 | 293 | 176 | 2,321 | 5,960 |
| (4) Indirect taxes *less* subsidies | 1,630 | 305 | 1,371 | 52 | 114 | — | 1,537 | 3,472 |
| (5) Incomes and depreciation | 8,857 | 17,780 | — | — | — | — | — | 26,637 |
| (6) Total input | 17,133 | 22,876 | 20,049 | 5,082 | 5,121 | 5,817 | 36,069 | 76,078 |

intermediate sales and purchases and hence the measures of total output and input. Thus, in Table 8*a*, all transactions between firms

[1] The figures in this table are adapted from Table 19 of *National Income and Expenditure, 1966*.

within the manufacturing sector have been 'netted out' since the input-output table distinguishes only transactions across sector boundaries. Similarly, Table 8*a* excludes transactions within the non-manufacturing sector. The Blue Book table, from which our table has been derived, distinguishes seven sub-sectors within the manufacturing sector and seven within the non-manufacturing sector and so records all transactions between these sub-sectors, a portion of them being within our manufacturing sector or within our non-manufacturing sector. This is the reason why the Blue Book table shows total output or input at £81,054m; this is £4,976m higher than the corresponding figure of our Table 8*a*, £3,280m being transactions within the manufacturing sector and £1,696m within the non-manufacturing sector. If even more industrial sectors in the economy were to be shown, a greater amount of intermediate transactions would be recorded and total input or output would have a higher value. At the other extreme, with only one sector, the input-output table would become very similar to the national income matrix set out in Table 5*b*.

An input-output table does little more than provide us with some interesting information about the structure of the economy in a past period. True, a series of such tables for successive years might be useful for policy purposes, both at the governmental and individual business level, if only because it would provide us with orders of magnitude which could not be readily guessed at. But the table would be much more useful if it could be used to illustrate the probable effects of changes occurring in individual sectors on the rest of the economy. For this, however, we have to assume or establish technical relationships between the physical outputs of the different sectors and the physical inputs absorbed by them. This brings us face to face with a problem of economic theory, just as we found in the previous chapter.

### 3. *The theoretical problem*

The usual first approximation found in the discussion of the Leontief system is that *output in each industry is proportional to each input*. For example, if 200 units of a given product are produced with 50 units of input A and 25 units of input B, then it is assumed that, say, an expansion of output to 400 units would call forth a demand for 100 units of input A and 50 of input B. Thus output is proportional to each input or, in other words, factors are combined in fixed proportions. It is also implicitly assumed that marginal output is proportional to each marginal input. Provided we can assume that prices are constant, we can express this relationship in money values. In our example, let us assume that units of output sell at one shilling per unit, inputs of A are purchased at two shillings per unit and of B at four shillings per unit. Then, with constant prices, an increase of 200 shillings in the money value of the final product will produce increases at 100 shillings each in the money values of inputs A and B.

Now let us take the table for 1963 given in the previous section and consider, for instance, what would happen if exports by the manufacturing sector were to increase by £300m and there were no other changes in the demand of final buyers and no change in the rate of indirect taxes. Before embarking on any calculations, let us note in qualitative terms what the consequences will be. First, total output by manufacturing will certainly rise by at least the £300m of extra export demand. But this additional output will itself entail extra demand by the manufacturing sector for the intermediate output of the non-manufacturing sector. And in turn, the extra required output of the non-manufacturing sector will entail increased intermediate demand upon the manufacturing sector. So it is clear that an increase of £300m in final demand on the manufacturing sector will imply a rise of more than £300m in manufacturing output, and also an increase in non-manufacturing output, and consequential changes in imports and factor incomes.

Now we turn to the calculation. In principle, it could be followed through by the iterative process which is implicit in the approach of the last paragraph. But it is more simply carried through by setting down the equations which must be satisfied by the various input and output values in our system and then solving the equations by the usual algebraic method. The calculation is carried out in two stages. First, we calculate the effect on the outputs of our two sectors of the given increase in final demand on one of them. Secondly, we follow through the consequences of these changes on imports, taxes and factor incomes.

For the manufacturing sector, let

$I_1$ be the value of intermediate purchases from the non-manufacturing sector,

$F_1$ be the total final demand on the sector,

and $T_1$ be the value of total output.

A similar notation, with the suffix 2, will be used for the non-manufacturing sector.

Now we note from the input-output table that, for every 100 units of total output of the manufacturing sector, 24 units (4,119 : 17,133) are purchased as intermediate output from the other sector. Hence we have the relation

$$I_1 = \cdot 240T_1$$

$$\text{Similarly } I_2 = \cdot 161T_2$$

where ·161 is the ratio 3,679 : 22,876.

$$\text{But } I_2 + F_1 = T_1$$

because the total output of manufacturing is equal to the intermediate purchases by the non-manufacturing sector ($I_2$) plus the final demand for manufacturing output ($F_1$).

$$\text{Similarly } I_1 + F_2 = T_2$$

$$\text{Hence} \quad \left.\begin{aligned} \cdot 161T_2 + F_1 &= T_1 \\ \cdot 240T_1 + F_2 &= T_2 \end{aligned}\right\} \quad \text{(A)}$$

The equations (A) are two equations in two unknowns $T_1$ and $T_2$ which can be solved for $T_1$ and $T_2$ if values are specified for $F_1$ and $F_2$. In our present example, we are told that

$$\begin{aligned} F_1 &= 13{,}454 + 300 \\ &= 13{,}754 \\ \text{and } F_2 &= 18{,}757 \end{aligned}$$

and so we solve the equations

$$\begin{aligned} \cdot 161T_2 + 13{,}754 &= T_1 \\ \cdot 240T_1 + 18{,}757 &= T_2 \end{aligned}$$

$$\text{giving } T_1 = 17{,}444 \text{ and } T_2 = 22{,}951.$$

$$\begin{aligned} \text{Hence } I_1 &= 22{,}951 - 18{,}757 = 4{,}194 \\ \text{and } I_2 &= 17{,}444 - 13{,}754 = 3{,}690. \end{aligned}$$

The actual 1963 situation can now be compared with the output situation on the assumption of an extra £300m export demand on the manufacturing sector. We do this by summarising rows (1) and (2) of the input-output table and showing the new situation in brackets (Table 8*b* overleaf). It will be seen that manufacturing output would increase, not by £300m, but by £311m and output of the non-manufacturing sector by £75m.

Passing on to the second stage, we calculate the effect on imports, taxes and factor incomes assuming, as before, constant

TABLE 8*b*

| Sales by | Intermediate purchases by Manufacturing | Intermediate purchases by Non-manufacturing | Purchases by final buyers | Total Output |
|---|---|---|---|---|
| Manufacturing | — | 3,679 | 13,454 | 17,133 |
| | (—) | (3,690) | (13,754) | (17,444) |
| Non-manufacturing | 4,119 | — | 18,757 | 22,876 |
| | (4,194) | (—) | (18,757) | (22,951) |

proportions of inputs. Manufacturing input has increased by a factor 17,444 : 17,133 = 1.018 and non-manufacturing input by 22,951 : 22,876 = 1.003. By applying these factors to the 1963 values of the inputs, we arrive at the following table showing the changes in terms of columns (1) and (2) of the input-output table:

TABLE 8*c*

| Sales by | Purchases by Manufacturing | Purchases by Non-manufacturing |
|---|---|---|
| (1) Manufacturing | — | 3,679 |
| | (—) | (3,690) |
| (2) Non-manufacturing | 4,119 | — |
| | (4,194) | (—) |
| (3) Imports | 2,527 | 1,112 |
| | (2,573) | (1,116) |
| (4) Indirect taxes less subsidies | 1,630 | 305 |
| | (1,659) | (306) |
| (5) Incomes and depreciation | 8,857 | 17,780 |
| | (9,018) | (17,839) |
| (6) Total input | 17,133 | 22,876 |
| | (17,444) | (22,951) |

We can now record some of the main changes which would take place in the economy, given our assumptions (Table 8*d*).

We see clearly that the effect of an expansion of exports purchased from Manufacturing is not by any means confined to that sector. First of all, as we see from row 3 of Table 8*d*, it promotes an increase in the demand for inputs from the other sector; this in turn produces a small further increase in demand for the output of the original sector, Manufacturing, as we see from row 2, where the expansion of output in manufacturing exceeds the increase in sales to final buyers listed in row 1. If we turn to examine the effects on the level of national income, we see that the original expansion of exports by £300m produces an expansion in total incomes of £220m (aggregate of row 6) and of imports by £50m (aggregate of row 4).

TABLE 8*d*

| | Manufacturing | Non-manufacturing | Total |
|---|---|---|---|
| | £m | £m | £m |
| (1) Increase in Sales to Final Buyers | 300 | — | 300 |
| (2) Increase in Output | 311 | 75 | 386 |
| (3) Increase in Purchase of Inputs from other sectors within industry | 75 | 11 | 86 |
| (4) Increase in Purchases of Imports | 46 | 4 | 50 |
| (5) Increase in net Indirect Taxes | 29 | 1 | 30 |
| (6) Increase in Purchases of Factor Services[1] | 161 | 59 | 220 |

Our calculation has related to the repercussions of an increase of £300m in export demand for manufacturing goods. But it will be clear that the calculations would have been the same if the increased demand for manufactures had come from any other category of final buyer. Also, if instead we had assumed an increase in export demand of £100m, one-third of the figure which was used, the computed changes in output would also be one-third of those actually calculated. (This follows from the nature of equations (A)). The following more general statement can therefore be made from our calculations: for every £100m increase in final demand on the manufacturing sector, output of manufacturing will increase by about £104m (one-third of £311m) and output of non-manufacturing will increase by £25m (one-third of £75m). Moreover, we could, by the same method, evaluate the effects of an increase of £100m in final demand on the

[1] Including depreciation.

non-manufacturing sector. Without going through the arithmetic here, the result is that output of the non-manufacturing sector would increase by £104m and output by the manufacturing sector by £17m. The table sums up these results.

*Total requirements of sector output per £100m of demand by final buyers*

Values in £m

| | Final demand on: Manufacturing | Non-manufacturing |
|---|---|---|
| Required output of: | | |
| Manufacturing | 104 | 17 |
| Non-manufacturing | 25 | 104 |

Each entry in this matrix represents the required output of the 'row' sector in which it lies for every £100m of final demand on the 'column' sector in which it lies. The process by which we arrive at this table from the original input-output matrix is known as 'inverting the matrix'.[1] A table on the same lines specifying all the sub-sectors of production is given in the national income Blue Book. Its value will be clear. From it, one can easily calculate the effect on sector outputs of any predetermined change in final demand on one or more sectors.

This analysis is complementary with the Keynesian analysis. Thus, in the case of an expansion of exports resulting in the generation of further factor incomes it would be unrealistic to assume, for example, that the purchase of final output by households at constant prices would remain fixed and therefore this problem and related problems discussed in Chapter 7 would have to be considered in any policy recommendations. In other words, the input-output theory would have to be extended to deal, not only with inter-industry relationships, but also with the kind of inter-sector relationships described by the Keynesian type of model. Another factor in this investigation of the various inter-relationships in the economy which the input-output approach brings to light, and which is not explicit in the Keynesian approach, is the change in the *proportions* of income in the different sectors and sub-sectors generated by a given change in output. This may throw some light on the distribution of incomes brought about through inter-industry relationships, which is of importance in considering the effect of changes in different kinds of expenditure on the demand for final output by households.

But a word of warning is necessary. The example we have chosen

[1] This is a term which comes from the matrix algebra method of solving simultaneous linear equations.

is only a crude first approximation. We assumed that no price changes would follow from the £300m expansion in exports. This means that any expansion would have to come about through an increase in the amount of labour supplied, e.g. by longer hours of work at constant wage rates. Again, in the short run, at least, increases in inputs of raw materials could be made by running down stocks of goods. This suggests that our simple theory of production needs to be modified to take account of stock changes and the relationships between stocks of goods and flows of inputs and outputs. Nor does the example allow for varying intensity in the use of capital equipment. Moreover, the possibility that prices may change both relatively and absolutely raises the whole question of the stability of the assumed relationship between outputs and inputs, quite apart from the difficulty of converting physical relationships into money values in our input-output table. Can we really assume that the proportions of factors employed will not be affected by changes in relative prices? Even in the short run, this is doubtful. These are some of the matters which call for further investigation and which are at present the subject of research. We cannot discuss the further developments of this analysis here, but our exposition perhaps gives some idea of the way in which the older 'general equilibrium' analysis has been given an empirical content, and how it can be used to extend our general understanding of the effects of given courses of action.

# Part III

# Further analysis

# 9

# THE CONCEPTUAL BASIS OF NATIONAL INCOME ACCOUNTS

## 1. *Introduction*

We saw in Chapter 1 that national income accounting is concerned with describing the economic activity of a region as the first step towards a fuller understanding of the general nature and effects of that activity. Anyone interested in this topic is, however, faced with a problem that sooner or later is bound to beset almost every person engaged in the systematic pursuit of knowledge. The problem is as follows. The facts with which we are concerned in most fields of knowledge are many in number and exhibit great complexity in their relationships, one with another. To know in detail all the facts relating to a particular study and to be able to trace their individual relationships would be normally impossible for any person, however industrious; nor, even assuming that these facts and relationships could all be known, would it be possible for most human minds to interpret such a complex mass of data as they would represent. It seems to be the natural reaction of the human mind in such circumstances to classify, with varying degrees of precision, depending upon the man and the nature of the problem, the relevant facts and relationships into a sufficiently small number of categories for them to be comprehended and considered together, after which they can be used as a basis for judgments about the nature of the world and its inhabitants; and, perhaps, for purposes of prediction. The various arrangements and classifications of data which fall under the head of social accounting are an example in the field of economics of this human phenomenon.

But the very process of classifying and thus simplifying the raw data of life introduces new difficulties. The price we have to pay for the gain in ease of handling problems is loss of precision in description and a restriction in the field within which any generalisations or predictions are valid, for either we must restrict what we say of the members of a class of data to what is common to all the data in that class (which may be too trivial to be of interest) or we shall have to make statements about the class which can guide us in our general understanding yet are in degrees untrue when applied to individual members of the class. In the natural sciences this problem has not been a serious one; for it has been found that the circumstances in which inaccuracies about individual phenomena within a class may be ignored for practical purposes can usually be clearly recognised. A prediction accurate enough for normal engineering purposes can, for example, be made by using Newtonian mechanics, though this in fact involves mis-statements about certain phenomena which are important in the investigation of, for example, certain astronomical problems.

In economics the problem is more serious, for although the same approach as in the natural sciences is perfectly justified in principle, and is in fact adopted, it is much less easy to see clearly when the effects of generalisation will lead to bad decisions. This is partly because in economic matters the data and relationships are constantly changing and the investigations can seldom be controlled and repeated under similar conditions, so that the conclusions cannot be checked; and partly because the studies are concerned with *human* behaviour and welfare so that generalisations about a class of facts that are not true of individual facts which are members of that class may sometimes lead to action or inaction which prejudices *people*. Few people, for example, would be prepared to accept as expressing a satisfactory state of affairs the statement that 'Homeless people do not in general starve to death in England' if they believed this statement concealed the fact that 5 per cent of homeless people *did* in fact starve to death, though in engineering a 5 per cent tolerance may be good enough for a particular operation. In economic studies, then, particular care is needed that the particular is not completely lost sight of in the general, necessary as the latter concept is.

We shall attempt, therefore, in this part of the book to make it somewhat easier for readers to understand how the rather abstract concepts discussed in Part I are related to the economic life of the community. It is hoped to draw attention in particular to a question which, though it is not normally overlooked by informed people who make use of the conceptual apparatus of the national income accounts, is, by reason of the way in which the national income data is presented, not always immediately obvious to students.

The point we refer to is the importance of considering movements in the various kinds of assets and liabilities of transactors, as distinct from the study of income and expenditure and other transfers, which are an analysis of the net effect of these movements. Indeed, it is not too much to say that until national income accounts are so drafted as to indicate movements in quantity and value of classes of assets and goods they will remain in some respects inadequate vehicles for clear thought and planning. This is another way of saying that a consideration of asset structure changes is an essential in appreciating the way in which the concepts of social accounting are related to the complex system of markets and price-relationships with which the main body of economic thought is concerned.

In Part I it was shown how the activity in a national region may, for study purposes, be conveniently divided into functional classes, under heads which we called 'firms', 'households' and 'government'. The quantities recorded represent 'command over resources' passing to and fro, and though this 'flow of value' does not correspond in all respects to an actual money flow in the economy, it can, by making certain assumptions about the rearrangement of assets in the various sectors, be pictured in that way. We now propose to investigate in greater detail the conceptual link between these measurements and the individual transactions which they symbolise. In order to do this we shall adopt the plan of examining the activities of hypothetical individual transactors in two of our sectors. This does not, of course, imply that all members of each sector are alike: far from it. It will be for readers to develop this line of thought with such applications as they choose. Our investigation will also provide a basis for the study of the asset structure of the whole economy, which is the subject of Chapter 10.

As we shall be concerned with assets and liabilities it is as well to start by considering briefly what we mean by these. Assets fall into two classes, 'goods' and 'claims'. Liabilities are 'claims'. By goods we mean physical 'things' which are under the control of people and have for the time being the qualities both of being wanted by people, for one reason or another, and of being 'scarce'—that is, of not being available without sacrifice by *someone*. Claims are socially recognised property which may be wanted and have value not because they are capable in any physical sense of satisfying wants, or of providing the means of satisfying wants, but because they are in the nature of *promises* which sooner or later are expected to lead, perhaps (as in the case of money) at a time chosen by the owner, to the acquisition of goods and services. It is characteristic of claims that to a man living on a desert island, with no contact with the outside world, they could never be of use, for they depend for their value on undertakings made by other people in the same economic community (which may, in some respects at least, transcend national barriers). For the same reason, claims given by members of a given economic region to others in that region cannot, unlike claims on *other* regions, be counted as part of the economic wealth of the region *taken as a whole* (except in the limited sense that a well-functioning money and credit system is an indispensable aid to effective division of labour in a modern community so that the loss of the system as a whole would certainly cause a loss of wealth to the community). To individual members of a community, however, claims are valuable resources, and their acquisition, sacrifice and possession are of great significance in the study of economic behaviour. Liabilities are claims looked at from the point of view of the promisor, whose wealth is correspondingly reduced by the promise he has made, and they may, therefore, be regarded as negative assets. Money is a very special type of claim. When in its usual modern form of bank notes or bank deposits it is in a formal legal sense the liability of the issuing bank or government. For practical purposes, so long as it is freely accepted in payment, it is a general claim on the resources of the community. Other typical claims are trade debts and stocks and shares.

2. *The accounts of persons*

We shall begin our investigation with 'households'. This sector is concerned with the activities of persons resident in the area studied in their capacity of recipients of income from the sale of personal and other factor services, recipients of transfers, and disposers of the command over resources thus placed in their hands. Let us imagine a person—let us call him *A*—and consider how his non-business economic activities might be recorded, were he to keep accounts, and investigate how such records would be conceptually related to the account of the household sector of the national income statistics. In this way we shall hope to obtain a clearer insight into the significance of the national statistics and of the relations of the transactions of one sector with the rest of the economy.

Let us suppose that at the beginning of a certain year *A* has the following assets and liabilities: clothes and other personal possessions, a motor-car, a house, £200 on current account at the bank and £20 in notes and coin, a balance of £400 in the Post Office Savings Bank, 1,000 ordinary shares in an industrial company, 100 bonds issued by a foreign government, a life assurance policy, and a loan of £1,000 from a building society.

Let us also suppose that during the year *A*: lives in his own house; receives in money £1,000 (after deduction of income tax) for services rendered in his job with a company carrying on a manufacturing business; receives £10 interest on his savings deposit which he withdraws in cash; receives £55 dividend (after deduction of income tax) from his shares; receives £30 interest (also after tax) from his foreign government bond; and pays £60 interest to his building society. He also sells his shares at the end of the year for £2,000 and repays £600 of his building society loan. His personal expenditure for his family and himself is £1,700. He also buys a new motor-car for £900 and receives £200 on the sale of the old one. He pays the annual premium of £200 on his life assurance policy. We will assume that he ends up with a similar collection of personal possessions to those at the beginning of the year, with £40 at the bank, £15 in hand, and other possessions unchanged.

*A* will probably not need much in the way of accounts to tell him what has happened to his economic position during the year, but he will probably have in his mind some kind of picture of his belongings at the beginning and end of the year, whether he writes it down on paper or not. If we write this down we shall have two balance sheets, drawn up in terms of *quantities*, rather than values, like this:

*Balance sheets at beginning and end of year*

| *Beginning* | *End* |
|---|---|
| *Assets* | *Assets* |
| Clothes and personal possessions | Clothes and personal possessions |
| Old motor-car | New motor-car |
| House | House |
| £200 at bank | £40 at bank |
| £20 in hand | £15 in hand |
| £400 at post office | £400 at post office |
| 1,000 shares in industrial company | — |
| 100 bonds of foreign government | 100 bonds of foreign government |
| Life assurance policy | Life assurance policy |
| *Liability* | *Liability* |
| £1,000 owing to building society | £400 owing to building society |

*A* will also have, no doubt, a record capable of being put into the form called by accountants a cash account, but which we will call 'money account', which will record his money transactions and explain the net change in his money holding over the year, like this:

*Money account*

| *Receipts* | £ | *Payments* | £ |
|---|---|---|---|
| Salary (less tax) | 1,000 | Interest paid to building society | 60 |
| Interest on savings deposit | 10 | Repayment of building society loan | 600 |
| Dividend on shares (less tax) | 55 | Expenditure on consumption | 1,700 |
| Interest on foreign bonds (less tax) | 30 | Cost of new car less proceeds of old | 700 |
| Sale of shares | 2,000 | Life assurance premium | 200 |
| Total | 3,095 | Total | 3,260 |
| | | Net change = decrease in balance at bank and in hand | 165 |

For *A*'s own purposes this method of presenting the information about his economic position at the beginning and end of the year, and the changes in money holdings, is probably adequate. But we are now considering *A* as one member of a large class of people.

Let us consider how the compiler of national income accounts arranges the data relating to *A*'s transactions. We are not, of course, suggesting that the statistician will really build up his totals by first collecting from *A*, and from everyone else, their personal and business accounts, and then putting these accounts together. We are, however, writing *as if* he collected his figures in this way because, thereby, we can more easily demonstrate the significance of his aggregates. Moreover some of the statistician's figures, for example, in the business sector, *are* ultimately derived from individual accounting records, and the statistics cannot be fully appreciated without some knowledge of how these records are prepared. We shall find that in his arrangement of the figures, the statistician follows much the same procedure as *A* would himself if he were setting out all the data in full double-entry book-keeping style, as a business man would have to do if it were a matter of business transactions, and as *A* himself might do if he were wealthy enough (or meticulous enough) to consider detailed accounting worthwhile. On the other hand, we shall find that the national income statistician selects only part of the picture that would be presented by such a set of double-entry accounts and omits the rest, and also makes certain additions and adjustments to the figures.

A book-keeping system, in essentials, is merely a systematic way of recording and classifying, in terms of values, (*a*) additions to, and deductions from, a collection of assets and liabilities, and (*b*) changes in values of members of that collection to the extent that these are considered worthwhile recording. Each type of asset or liability is classified by assigning it to an *account*. The convention for recording changes in value is the same as that we used in the money account above: in the case of assets, additions to wealth, whether due to changes in quantity or in value per unit, are recorded on the left-hand (debit) side and deductions on the right-hand (credit) side. Liabilities are treated as negative assets so that *additions* are recorded on the right-hand side and deductions on the left-hand side. Thus, if, for each class of property, we did what we have done in the money account in respect of *A*'s money transactions, we should have a set of accounts portraying the whole of his economic activity for the year: that is, we should have a picture of the flows of goods and claims, including money, to and from *A*, thus:

*Shares in industrial company*

| *Increase* | £ | *Decrease* | £ |
|---|---|---|---|
| | — | Sale of 1,000 shares for money | 2,000 |

*Loan from building society*

| *Decrease in loan* | £ | *Increase in loan* | £ |
|---|---|---|---|
| Amount repaid in money | 600 | | — |

*Motor-cars*

| *Increase* | £ | *Decrease* | £ |
|---|---|---|---|
| Purchase for money | 900 | Sale for money | 200 |

*Life assurance policy*

| *Increase in amount invested* | £ | *Decrease in amount invested* | £ |
|---|---|---|---|
| Annual premium paid in money | 200 | | — |

We need not trouble to record *A*'s acquisition and use of other goods and services, as we have assumed these would have no net effect on his position.

In practice, of course, a book-keeper would also record opening and closing balances, including those of accounts on which no movement had taken place (e.g. for the house), any net change in an account being given by the difference between the balance at the beginning and the balance at the end of the period. Here, as we are concerned only with events during the year, we record only the net changes.

A study of these accounts (including the money account) would remind *A* of the economic happenings during the year. There is, however, no single account which summarises in a clear way the over-all effect of these changes: that is to say, which records in one figure how much better or worse off *A* was at the end of the year, or shows the amount of the consumption he was able to enjoy during the year. Nor is there an account which provides a simple analysis in terms of types of economic activity of the rise and fall in his wealth during the year: how it was built up and expended.

Of course, in this simple case, *A* himself could, if he wanted, get a good enough idea of these things by means of back-of-envelope calculations. We are interested, however, in seeing how an accountant would introduce these refinements into the book-keeping system, for this will also give us the conceptual foundation of the national income figures. The arithmetic is easy enough. All *A* does, in effect, is to bring together all the changes in assets and liabilities recorded above in separate accounts, into one big account, cancel out on both sides of this account any items which merely represent an exchange of one asset or liability for another, and call the result an 'income account' or 'income and expenditure account'. Let us take the first step of 'consolidating' all the accounts we have listed above by setting out in one account (*a*) the left-hand and (*b*) the right-hand items of each separate account. We have:

| *Increases in wealth* | £ | *Decreases in wealth* | £ |
|---|---|---|---|
| Salary (less tax) | 1,000 | Interest paid to building society | 60 |
| Interest on savings deposit | 10 | Repayment of building society loan | 600 |
| Dividend on shares (less tax) | 55 | Expenditure on consumption | 1,700 |
| Interest on foreign bonds (less tax) | 30 | Net cost of new car | 700 |
| Sale of shares | 2,000 | Life assurance premium | 200 |
| Building society loan repaid | 600 | Shares sold | 2,000 |
| New car bought | 900 | Old car sold | 200 |
| Life insurance policy | 200 | | |
| Total | 4,795 | Total | 5,460 |
| | | Net change = decrease in wealth | 665 |

*A* thus seems to have *dissaved* £665, that is to say, decreases in his wealth which have not brought corresponding increases have exceeded by £665 increases not accompanied by corresponding decreases. At this point, however, we must make an adjustment to *A*'s accounts to bring the conventions on which they are prepared more into line with those used in national income statistics.

It will be noticed that the £700 net increase in *A*'s wealth represented by the difference between the value of the new and old motor-cars has been included in the account, and offsets the corresponding net money payment of £700. The motor-car transactions have thus not been allowed to affect the calculation of his net change in wealth. Now this may well be the way that *A* would look at the matter himself: assuming that he can sell the new car for the price paid, his total wealth has not been decreased by the transaction. However, as explained in Part I, national income statisticians assume, as a matter of convenience, that the purchase by final consumers of such goods as motor-cars is equivalent to an actual consumption of wealth, no allowance being made for the continued existence of the purchased asset at the end of the period in question, even at a partly worn-out value. Hence, if we are to bring *A*'s account strictly into line with aggregate statistics of which it conceptually forms part, we must eliminate the motor-car items from the accounts. There will no longer be a set-off of £700 'net increase in motor-cars' against the net money outlay on the new motor-car; the latter outlay will now form part of consumption expenditure, which will rise to £2,400. 'Dissaving' will be £700 higher at £1,365.

Our next step is to eliminate on both sides of the account the other items merely representing changes in the way in which *A* holds his wealth, so that we have what is called an 'income account':

*Income account*

| *Income* | £ | *Expenditure* | £ |
|---|---|---|---|
| Salary (less tax) | 1,000 | Interest paid to building society | 60 |
| Interest on savings deposit | 10 | Expenditure on consumption | 2,400 |
| Dividend on shares (less tax) | 55 | | |
| Interest on foreign bonds (less tax) | 30 | | |
| | 1,095 | | 2,460 |
| | | Net change = dissaving | 1,365 |

(It may be added that, unlike some national income statisticians, accountants take the final step of reversing the sides of the income account, so that increases in wealth are on the right-hand side and decreases on the left-hand side. This practice, which sometimes tends to confuse laymen, arises purely out of the traditional arithmetic of double-entry book-keeping and has no other significance. It is followed in the national income accounts of the United States. We should, perhaps, here comment that in showing the construction of the income account we have described the final *effect* of the accountant's entries, not his actual day-to-day procedure, for which any standard text-book on double-entry book-keeping may be consulted.)

*A*'s income account is now beginning to show signs of its relationship with the households account of Part I, of which it is conceptually part. On the left-hand side, the salary is part of incomes from the sale of factor services to firms. The interest on savings deposit is part of transfer payments from government. The dividend is part of profit distributed by firms. On the right-hand side, expenditure on consumption is part of purchases of consumption goods and services from firms. The building society interest is not represented in our earlier accounts: it represents a transfer payment to firms. In the aggregate accounts it will be deducted from interest paid to persons by firms. This leaves the interest received on foreign bonds. This, too, is not represented explicitly in our earlier system of accounts. As explained in Chapter 3 it represents a transfer payment from the firms or production sector, in which, in the United Kingdom, all current receipts from overseas other than gifts, whether from sale of exports or so-called 'invisible' items, are recorded as income.

Some further adjustments are, however, necessary.

Owing to a peculiarity of United Kingdom income tax law, certain types of income are subjected to tax by deduction, before they reach the recipient. It is customary in national income accounting, as in ordinary accounting, to record such receipts as they would have been had the income been received 'gross' and the tax subsequently handed over to the government. This is done by adding the amount of tax to both the income side and the expenditure side of the account. Let us assume that the tax deducted from *A*'s salary was £300; from the dividend was £45; and from the foreign interest was £25. Then these three items will appear on the income side of the account as £1,300 (1,000+300), £100 (55+45) and £55 (30+25), and there will be a corresponding new 'payment' of £370 on tax. The actual transfers of money will have been from the original payers to the central government. The current tax payments that have been made, or that are due, by or from firms will, in the firms account, be reduced by any such notional payments shown in the households account, and 'payments' of income by firms to households will be increased correspondingly.

Again, as we mentioned in Chapter 1, the ownership of houses is regarded as a productive activity to be classified with 'firms'. Hence the national income statisticians assume *A* has received an imputed 'income' from his house based on an estimate of its rental value (in the United Kingdom the tax assessment is used) less his outlay on repairs, and they assume *A* has incurred an 'expenditure' on consumption of an amount equal to the rental value of the house. Let us assume that the rental value was £62 and the repairs were £12. Then in *A*'s income account we must insert both a 'payment' of £50 and a 'receipt' of £50 for which there is no corresponding movement of assets. (We only have to record £50 additional payment for we assume his consumption expenditure already includes the £12 spent on repairs.) His 'savings' will thus be unchanged.

(In the United Kingdom *A* would also be liable to pay income tax directly to the Inland Revenue authorities on his bank deposit interest, £10, and, and prior to 1963, on the imputed net annual value of his house, £50. This liability would, in this example, be just offset by *A*'s right to deduct his building society interest of £60 from his total income for tax purposes. Hence we can assume there is no other tax liability.)

The amended account is now as follows:

*Income account*

| | £ | | £ |
|---|---|---|---|
| Salary [1,000+300] | 1,300 | Interest paid to building society | 60 |
| Interest on savings deposit | 10 | Expenditure on consumption [2,400+50] | 2,450 |
| Dividends [55+45] | 100 | Taxation [300+45+25] | 370 |
| Interest on foreign bonds [30+25] | 55 | | |
| Rent | 50 | | |
| | 1,515 | | 2,880 |
| | | Net change = dissaving | 1,365 |

It will noticed that for purposes of exposition we have been showing saving or dissaving as a net excess of receipts over payments or of payments over receipts, instead of as a payment to, or receipt from, capital account. If we arrange *A*'s income account in the form in which the aggregate income account of households appears in the summary tables of the United Kingdom National Income Blue Books (in which, however, it is called 'Personal Income and Expenditure') we have:

*Income account*

| | £ | | £ |
|---|---|---|---|
| Salary | 1,300 | Expenditure on consumption | 2,450 |
| Net interest [10−60] | −50 | Taxation | 370 |
| Dividend | 100 | Saving | −1,365 |
| Rent | 50 | | |
| Income from abroad | 55 | | |
| | 1,455 | | 1,455 |

To conform with the convention which we have discussed in Part I of regarding saving as 'paid' to, or dissaving as 'received' from, the capital account, an item equal to the balance on the income account is entered. (This item is shown on the right-hand side whether negative or positive in order that the left-hand side may record, in the aggregate accounts, total personal income. For the same reason 'Net interest' appears on the left-hand side.)

How is *A*'s income account related to his over-all economic position as recorded by his successive balance sheets? We have already shown that the income account is derived by listing changes in the value of *A*'s assets and liabilities. Hence it must follow that the net difference between *A*'s income and expenditure—his saving or dissaving—must be equal to—is, in fact, a way of describing—the net change in the value of his assets less his liabilities. If instead of merely preparing balance sheets in the form of simple inventories, as we did above, we record *A*'s economic position at the beginning and end of the year in terms of *values* his balance sheets might appear as follows:

| | *Beginning* £ | *End* £ |
|---|---|---|
| House at cost to *A* | 5,000 | 5,000 |
| Bank balance | 200 | 40 |
| Cash in hand | 20 | 15 |
| Post Office deposit | 400 | 400 |
| Shares in industrial company at market value | 2,000 | — |
| Foreign bonds at market value | 500 | 500 |
| Life assurance policy (amount of total premiums paid) | 400 | 600 |
| Total assets | 8,520 | 6,555 |
| Debt to building society | 1,000 | 400 |
| Net assets | 7,520 | 6,155 |

(It will be noted that the convention discussed above requires that all the personal possessions, including the motor-cars, should be excluded from these balance sheets: they are assumed, as it were, to have disappeared when they were bought by the final consumer.)

The difference in value between the two balance sheets is the £1,365 we have recorded in the income account for dissaving. This must follow from our method of preparing the income account.

Readers will notice we have, in preparing the balance sheets in value terms, introduced the assumption that *A* does not revalue any of his property while he holds it. Any change in his assessment of values would be a 'capital' profit or loss and hence excluded from the national accounts, as we noted in Chapter 4. In the same way we have assumed that the value *A* set on the shares at the beginning of the year is the same as the price which he received when he sold his shares. If there was, for example, a realised 'capital profit' because the sales value exceeded an earlier valuation this would not be recorded for national income purposes, though, of course, *A* might bring it into his own books.

A word of explanation is necessary with respect to the life assurance policy. Strictly speaking, we should increase the value of the policy over the year, not only by the amount of the money *A* has passed to the life office (which will have increased the life office's assets) but by *A*'s share (reflected in a higher present value of his policy) in the interest earned by the life office on its invested funds. We have ignored this in *A*'s accounts.

We have now seen that the net balance of *A*'s income account records the change in value (excluding 'capital' profits and losses) of his assets and liabilities, and this links up with our statement in Chapter 1 that the national income accounts, of which *A*'s income account is a conceptual part, record flows not necessarily of *money* but of *value*. When, however, we examine *A*'s income account we find that all the items in it *do* represent movements of *money* to or from *A*, with the exception of the taxation adjustment and the imputed house rent. In fact, income accounts of households tend to approximate more closely to a record of money transactions than do those of the other sectors. It will be noticed, however, that the income account does not record *all A*'s money transactions: it is *not* the same as his money account. We could also elaborate our system by assuming that during the year *A* incurred debt, or increased existing debt, with, for example, traders or hire-purchase finance companies for goods supplied to him. In this case part of the consumption expenditure in his income account would represent, not a money payment, but a rise in a liability.

This brings us to the important question of the meaning of the saving item (the balance of the income account) in relation to the economy as a whole. A satisfactory consideration of this demands the study of the relation of all the transactions of one sector with those of the other sectors. This we leave to be dealt with in Chapter 10. In anticipation of a more detailed examination of this problem, however, we may summarise the way in which *A* has financed his dissaving of £1,365. This dissaving has only been possible because *A* was able to draw on claims which he had at the beginning of the period.

Let us refer back to *A*'s asset and liability accounts (as distinct from his income account). We find that *A* has converted the shares in the industrial company into £2,000 in money. *A*'s sacrifice of this claim must mean that someone else has acquired it, and has surrendered money. In the case of the building society repayment *A* has parted with one type of claim, money, and thereby reduced equally the building society's claim on him. Finally *A* has sacrificed money in return for an increase in the value of the type of claim we call an assurance policy. The net result of these rearrangements of resources left *A* with additional money, but, on balance, fewer other claims. With this money, plus some reduction in his original cash balance, he has been able to devote to consumption expenditure more than his current 'income'.

It does not follow, of course, that *A* need part with *claims* in order to increase his money holding. He might, if he had them, sell *goods*: for example, his house.

Another point that merits attention is the fact that *A* need not necessarily own claims on someone else before he can increase his money holdings by asset structure changes. If he is credit-worthy he may, as suggested above, be able to *create* claims on himself, for example by purchasing goods on credit, just as a business can create its own securities. Consumption might also be 'financed', not by *A* first selling an asset for money and then spending the money, but by passing over assets in direct exchange for consumption goods, as might happen in a primitive economy, or in a developed economy in which the money had become mistrusted through continued inflation. In this case consumption expenditure would, in *A*'s books, be recorded as a right-hand item in the account of the asset concerned and would, as before, be absorbed into the income account when the latter was built up from the asset and liability accounts.

In *A*'s case we have assumed that over-spending of income (dis-saving) is taking place so that *A* requires finance. In other cases however, and probably in aggregate, the opposite will be true. We should find that receipts recorded in the income account had exceeded payments. The difference, to the extent that it was represented by a money balance, might have been retained in money form, e.g. as a bank balance, or held in notes; alternatively it might have been used to buy other assets. *The income account thus makes no distinction between different methods of financing,* and this is one of the weaknesses of national income accounting as a description of economic activity. In a developed economy financial transactions are of very great importance.

Before we leave *A* we shall consider one further complication arising from the fact that, in the United Kingdom classification, incomes of households (persons) include the profits of non-corporate businesses carried on by sole traders and partners. The profits for a given period represent the net change in value (on certain conventional bases) of an assorted collection of assets. It follows from this that very little of the profit for a given year may be represented by an increased business *money* balance. Suppose that the £1,300 we have included in the above accounts for *A*'s salary is in fact not all salary, but as to £1,000 salary and as to £300 profit from a small private business. (We will assume the tax payable on salary and profit was £200 and £100 respectively.) Now, the detailed business transactions would no doubt be recorded by *A* in a separate set of business accounts. If *A* kept private accounts at all, he would probably bring his profits into these only to the extent that he had withdrawn them from the business in money or in kind. In the national income accounts, however, the whole profit for the year is assumed to be brought into his private accounts, i.e. into the household sector.

Moreover, for this purpose profit means the figure in *A*'s business accounts before deducting depreciation of fixed equipment and before paying income tax on the profit. This implies that if *A*'s personal books were drafted on national income lines the receipt of business profits would, to the extent that assets had not actually been withdrawn from the business by *A*, be recorded as an increase in his *claims*: in this case in respect of his *equity in the business*. (There is implied, of course, a corresponding record in the *business* accounts of an increase in claims *against* the business).

As regards the tax liability, to the extent that it is actually paid in money it must be assumed that the business has transferred a corresponding sum of money to *A* who has then paid the tax, or that *A* has paid the tax from his private cash balance and increased his claim against the business correspondingly. It must be noted, however, that business taxes are commonly payable *after* the period in which the profit has been earned. The tax of £100 on the business profits will therefore probably be recorded not as a cash payment but as an increase in claims against *A* (in this case the claim being the contingent right of the Inland Revenue). On the other hand there will probably have been an actual payment of money during the year in respect of tax on *last* year's profits. Suppose the latter payment had been £80. The £80 will be a claim by the Inland Revenue against *A* at the beginning of the year. This will be paid during the year, but at the end of the year £100 will be shown as a claim of the Inland Revenue in respect of tax on this year's profits. Hence the net outgo in respect of tax will be represented by an £80 decrease in money and by a £20 increase in liabilities (called a tax reserve in the account). In the United Kingdom national income statistics it is customary to indicate the extent to which the tax incurred in the year of the account has been paid in money by dividing the tax 'payments' into (*a*) *money payments* (in this case £80) and (*b*) increase (or decrease) in *tax reserves.*

The accounting entries in *A*'s personal accounts needed to record this rather complicated tax position and transfer of profit would, supposing *A* withdrew from the business just enough money to pay the tax, be as follows:

*Money account*

| *Increase* | £ | *Decrease* | £ |
|---|---|---|---|
| Part of gross business profit for year withdrawn in money | 80 | Tax paid in respect of last year's business profits | 80 |

*Equity interest in private business*

| *Increase* | £ | *Decrease* | £ |
|---|---|---|---|
| Part of gross profit for year (before deducting provision for depreciation) not withdrawn in money | 220 | | |
| | 220 | | — |
| Net change = increase in value of private business interest | 220 | | |

*Claim of Inland Revenue for tax*

| *Decrease* | £ | *Increase* | £ |
|---|---|---|---|
| Tax on last year's profit satisfied by money payment | 80 | Amount owing in respect of this year's profit | **100** |
| | 80 | | **100** |
| | | Net change = increase in tax reserve | 20 |

We must remember that we have decreased the net money receipts of our previous example by £200, the salary now being £800 after tax instead of £1,000 and that the tax adjustment on the salary, which appears on both sides of the account, is £200 instead of £300. Allowing for this, and adding in the items in the above accounts, our income account appears as follows, with the amended items shown in bold print:

*Income account*

| | £ | | £ |
|---|---|---|---|
| Salary [800 + 200] | **1,000** | Expenditure on consumption | 2,450 |
| Business profits [80 + 220] | **300** | Taxation: | |
| Net interest | −50 | Payments [270 + 80] | **350** |
| Dividend | 100 | Increase in reserve | **20** |
| Rent | 50 | | |
| Income from abroad | 55 | | |
| | 1,455 | | 2,820 |
| | | Net change = dissaving | 1,365 |

Of the total tax provision of £370 (£350 + £20) £100 is attributable to the business, made up of £80 included with the other money payments, plus the £20 increase in the tax reserve.

The discussion of the personal accounts of an imaginary individual has not covered every item which will be found in a typical set of published statistics. We hope it has, however, given readers some idea of the conceptual basis of this class of account and that students will be able, by turning to the published statistics and reading the explanatory notes provided with these, to appreciate more fully their meaning.

## 3. *The accounts of firms*

We shall now consider the type of activity classified under the head of 'firms' or 'production'. As indicated in Part I, the firms account summarises the results of activities concerned with the production of national wealth, including the holding of claims on the rest of the world that bring in interest or dividends. We must imagine the national firms or production accounts as the aggregation of individual accounts of people and organisations carrying on these activities. The contents of each of these accounts can be regarded, just as in *A*'s case, as a summary of changes in the holdings of assets and liabilities.

We shall take as our example a business company, *X Ltd*, the shares of which are held by the public at large, i.e. by households (persons). We shall not examine, as with *A*, the assets and liabilities of the company at the beginning and end of the year, but shall confine ourselves to the changes during the year, restricting ourselves to a relatively small number of items which must symbolise the very large number of individual changes of all kinds that occur inside actual businesses. As before, all positive changes in wealth (other than those by convention not recorded), whether increases in quantity of a given unit value, or increases in value of the same quantity, will be recorded on the left-hand side of accounts, and negative changes on the right-hand side.

Let us assume that at the end of our year we examine the asset and liability accounts of the company and find the following entries, all of which represent changes during the year:[1]

[1] Readers instructed in commercial accounting practice will already have noticed that we have departed in several respects from the usual conventions, though we have preserved the ultimate meaning of the accounts. If one is to avoid a lengthy preliminary examination of these conventions this procedure is almost essential when writing for non-accountants.

*Money*

| *Receipts* | £000 | *Payments* | £000 |
|---|---|---|---|
| (1) Sales of consumer goods to private persons at home | 885 | (6) Wages and salaries (including tax paid on behalf of employees) | 800 |
| (2) Sales of goods to other domestic firms | 115 | (7) Rent (including income tax paid on behalf of landlord) | 10 |
| (3) Sales of goods to overseas customers | 400 | (8) Purchases of goods and services from other firms | 200 |
| (4) Subsidy from government | 40 | (9) Purchases of goods from overseas suppliers | 110 |
| (5) Subscriptions by equity shareholders for new shares | 500 | (10) Interest on company's debenture loan (including tax paid on behalf of debenture holders) | 25 |
| | | (11) Dividends on company's shares | 105 |
| | | (12) Purchase tax and local rates | 350 |
| | | (13) Corporation tax on company's own profits and income tax on dividends | 275 |
| | 1,940 | | 1,875 |
| (14) Net change = rise in money at bank and in hand | 65 | | |

*Debts due from domestic non-business customers*

| *Increase* | £000 | *Decrease* | |
|---|---|---|---|
| (15) New debts incurred for sales of goods in excess of debts repaid = net change | 60[1] | | — |

*Debts due from government departments*

| *Increase* | £000 | *Decrease* | |
|---|---|---|---|
| (16) New debts incurred for sales of goods in excess of debts repaid = net change | 300[1] | | — |

[1] In commercial accounts the rise and fall of debts and liabilities would be shown and not merely the net change.

*Debts due from overseas customers*

| *Increase* | | *Decrease* | |
|---|---|---|---|
| | £000 | | |
| (17) New debts incurred for sales of goods in excess of debts repaid = net change | 45[1] | | — |

*Liabilities to domestic suppliers*

| *Decrease* | | *Increase* | |
|---|---|---|---|
| | | | £000 |
| | — | (18) New liabilities for purchases of goods and services in excess of liabilities repaid = net change | 20[1] |

*Liabilities to overseas suppliers*

| *Decrease* | | *Increase* | |
|---|---|---|---|
| | £000 | | |
| (19) Excess of liabilities repaid over new liabilities for goods supplied = net change | 30[1] | | — |

*Liabilities to Inland Revenue authorities*

| *Decrease* | | *Increase* | |
|---|---|---|---|
| | | | £000 |
| | — | (20) Excess of amount owing (or to be owing) for the year's income tax and corporation tax over amounts paid during year = net change | 35 |

*Stocks of raw materials, work-in-progress and finished goods*

| *Increase* | | *Decrease* | |
|---|---|---|---|
| | | | £000 |
| | — | (21) Excess of valuation of stocks at beginning of year over stocks at end of year = net change | 15 |

*Claim of equity shareholders on company ('liability' of the company to its own shareholders)*

| *Decrease* | | *Increase* | |
|---|---|---|---|
| | | | £000 |
| | — | (22) Rise in equity interest in respect of new money subscribed = net change | 500 |

[1] See footnote 1 on p. 157.

*Fixed capital equipment*

| *Increase* | £000 | *Decrease* |
|---|---|---|
| (23) Value of rise in quantity held (valuation based on prices paid for equipment bought at home and abroad and on payments to factors of production, excluding own profit, and for other inputs for equipment manufactured by the company) | 150 | — |

As in the case of *A*, the amalgamation of these accounts will give us a summary of the recorded over-all changes in wealth of the company during the year, which can then be simplified by eliminating changes in asset structure not relevant to productive activities which affect both sides of the set of accounts. In this way we shall be able to derive *X Ltd*'s equivalent of what, on the national scale, is the firms or production account. We shall here call it, for convenience, *X Ltd*'s income account, by analogy with *A*'s income account. (In United Kingdom commercial practice the account—rather different in form—would be called the trading and profit and loss account or the manufacturing, trading and profit and loss account. Income account is shorter and, as it happens, coincides with American commercial practice.)

Our accounts do not record the continuous day-to-day rise in holdings of goods as these are bought or manufactured—a rise which is accompanied by a fall in assets (or a rise in liabilities) due to 'payments' to factors of production, other firms and overseas suppliers; nor do the accounts record the similar day-to-day fall in wealth as the processed goods pass to customers, accompanied by a rise in money or debts. (This is one of the respects in which we have made *X Ltd*'s accounts simpler than they would actually be in commercial practice, where they *would* record in some detail this ebb and flow of goods.) Instead, it is as if we regarded net movements of value to factors of production and to suppliers of intermediate inputs as decreases in wealth; net movements of value from customers as increases; and took account of the fact that either some goods produced or acquired during the year had not been sold, or that more goods had been sold than produced or acquired, by recording the net rise or fall in stocks and capital equipment. We thus introduce into the income account as three separate groups of items the *net* movements of value to factors of production, and to other firms; the *net* movements of value from customers; and the *net* rise and fall in value of stock and capital equipment.

Let us now construct our income account, as we did with *A*, by putting together the left-hand and right-hand sides of the individual accounts and eliminating the items which merely represent changes in the form in which wealth is held. There is here only one such change—the increase in money resulting from an equal rise in shareholders' claims on the company—and we shall proceed directly to the income account, leaving out these two items. In the following account we show by means of the code number of each item how the items are derived from the individual accounts above:

*Income account of X Ltd*

| | *Increases in wealth* | £000 | | *Decreases in wealth* | £000 |
|---|---|---|---|---|---|
| 1+15 | Sales of consumer goods to private persons at home [885+60] | 945 | 6 | Wages and salaries | 800 |
| | | | 7 | Rent | 10 |
| 2 | Sales of goods to other domestic firms | 115[1] | 8+18 | Purchases of goods and services from other firms [200+20] | 220[1] |
| 16 | Sales of goods to government[2] | 300 | 9−19 | Purchases of goods and services from overseas suppliers [110−30] | 80 |
| 3+17 | Sales of goods to overseas customers [400+45] | 445 | 21 | Value of fall in quantity of stocks held | 15 |
| | | | 10 | Interest | 25 |
| 4 | Subsidies | 40 | 11 | Dividends | 105 |
| 23 | Value of rise in quantity of capital equipment held | 150 | 12 | Purchase tax and local rates | 350 |
| | | | 13 +20 | Corporation tax and income tax [275+35] | 310 |
| | | 1,995 | | | 1,915 |
| | Net change=company's saving | 80 | | | |

In commercial accounts, the £80,000 net balance of the income account—that is, the net increase in *X Ltd*'s wealth or 'undistributed profit'—would be treated as if it were a claim of *X Ltd*'s share-

[1] These items will cancel out with corresponding items in the accounts of other firms when the accounts are aggregated. From *X Ltd*'s point of view they do not cancel as they are part of the company's income and expenditure.

[2] We shall assume these sales represent current expenditure of government, and not the purchase of investment goods.

holders against the company. Indeed, one way of looking at the income account is as the 'liability' account of the business to the shareholders in respect of the profit earned for them, but not yet distributed to them. This is brought out very clearly by the customary practice of recording, in contrast with the other accounts, increases in the business wealth on the *right-hand* side and decreases on the *left-hand* side. In our income account this is not done—we are following the present practice of the United Kingdom statisticians, which we believe makes it easier to appreciate the true nature of an income account—so that the symmetry is rather spoilt, but we could achieve the same result by entering the £80,000 in a 'liability' account recording the increase in the shareholders' interest in the equity. The income account would then balance with zero saving. Our present treatment, on the other hand, is consistent with the idea that undistributed profit of companies is a special category of saving, and should not be regarded as a transfer to households. Admittedly, however, it involves a certain contradiction, for it implies that the saving does not 'belong' to anyone, or that it belongs to the company, which is a fictitious person. The existence of this contradiction reflects a vagueness in shareholders' interests which exists in real life.

In the calculation of *X Ltd*'s saving no deduction has been made for depreciation. The value of the rise in quantity of *X Ltd*'s fixed equipment *less* the fall in stocks would, in the national account, be called *gross* investment and not *net*. Were a deduction for depreciation made from this figure, the balance of the income account would be correspondingly reduced. In this respect our draft of *X Ltd*'s accounts for the purpose of national income accounting will differ from *X Ltd*'s own accounts which will include an allowance for depreciation.

The reader will remember from Chapter 4 that if there has been a general rise (or fall) in the price level, so that end of the year stock has been valued on the basis of a higher or lower price level than beginning of the year stock, it will be possible to regard the recorded stock change as consisting of a mixture of (*a*) a change in quantity of stock of given unit value (called 'value of physical increase or decrease'); and (*b*) a change in value, due to the price level rise or fall, of a given quantity (called 'stock appreciation' or 'depreciation'). It is customary to calculate an approximate figure indicating the size of (*b*) and to show this as a separate part of the increase or decrease in value of stocks held. It is then possible to give an estimate of how much of the profit—and therefore of the saving—is due only to general price level changes. Let us assume that if the physical quantities of stock at the beginning and end of the year were valued at the average price for the year, the fall in the value of the stock held by *X Ltd* would be £32,000. As the actual fall in value shown is only £15,000, we replace this net figure by the two figures of £32,000 'disinvestment in stocks' and £17,000 'stock appreciation'. The latter is not regarded as part of gross investment, so that if we are to maintain the consistency of our definitions laid down in Chapter 1, we should split our present savings figure into 'true savings' and 'spurious' savings due to stock appreciation. (Even 'true' savings are not savings in the original Keynesian sense, for they have not been reduced by a depreciation deduction.)

In the case of United Kingdom statistics a further point arises in connexion with company tax payments. Corporation tax is levied on a company's profits and paid by it. Moreover, the shareholders of a company are liable for income tax on their dividend receipts. This tax (computed at the standard rate) is also paid by the company to the Inland Revenue so that the shareholder receives the dividend net and has no more standard rate income tax to pay on it (though if he has a big enough income he may have to pay surtax). Just as in *A*'s income account we made a notional entry on both sides (which did not, therefore, have any net effect on *A*'s saving), so in *X Ltd*'s accounts we make an appropriate addition to the figure of dividends paid, to show them at the gross figure, and a corresponding reduction in the tax payment. In other words, we arrange the figures as if part of the transfer of money, or claim to money, to the Inland Revenue were in fact made to the recipients of the dividends who themselves accounted for the tax to the Revenue. Let us assume that the tax attributable to the net dividends paid by *X Ltd* is £86,000. This amount must, in our final table, be added to dividends and deducted from taxation. (It may be noted that businesses also pay over the income tax on wages, salaries, rent and interest to the Inland Revenue on behalf of the recipients. These payments have already been recorded in the money account as part of the payments made to (or for) these people and no further adjustment is, therefore, necessary. We have dealt with dividends differently because, unlike the other items, there is no direct connexion between deduction of the tax on payment of the dividends and payment of tax by the company to the Inland Revenue.)

Having noted these points, our next step is to show how *X Ltd*'s income account as we have prepared it, and incorporating the stock appreciation and income tax adjustments we have just mentioned, requires rearranging before it will fit neatly into the pattern currently used in the United Kingdom statistics.

The first step is to split the account into two parts which we may call the production, operating or trading account and the appropriation account, corresponding to what may be called the activity of *production* and the activity of administering, or *appropriating*, the resultant profits. The latter activity includes the allocation of profit between interest, dividends, taxation on profits and undistributed surplus or saving of the company.

It may be noted that a divergence between national income and commercial practice arises in connexion with 'interest'. 'Interest' represents the payment for borrowed money (e.g. debenture loans) as distinct from 'dividends', which are, in legal theory at least, a payment of a profit share to ownership (i.e. share) interests. In commercial accounts this interest is regarded as an expense, to be deducted *before* calculating profit, whereas in the national accounts it may be shown in the appropriation account as if paid *out of* profits. Neither treatment, of course, can be called 'right'. The definition of profit is a matter of convenience. (Interest in the above sense is not, of course, the same concept as the theoretical economist's 'interest', which is often used to cover *all* returns on invested funds, i.e. including 'dividends'.)

The arithmetic of the rearrangement is, as usual, very simple. The items allocated to the appropriation account are removed thereto. The reduced income account is renamed production, operating or trading account, and the items removed are replaced by one omnibus 'payment', just as if a claim—for example, money—had moved from the production account to the appropriation account. In the latter an equivalent 'receipt' is recorded. The two accounts taken together still represent the firms account of Part I.

In addition to splitting the account into two we have to rearrange the contents a little to make them fit more conveniently into the usual arrangements of the national accounts, and we have also to re-word the explanations of the figures. As in the case of *A*, this involves transferring one or two items to the opposite side of the account and adding a negative sign. We also divide the appropriation account itself into two sections, so that it shows the undistributed income of *X Ltd* (*a*) before and (*b*) after taxation. This split is, in miniature, a process like the original split between production and appropriation except that it is not thought worth while to separate the two sections of the appropriation account from one another and give them different names.

We now have (with altered figures in bold type):

*Production account of X Ltd*

| | £000 | | £000 |
|---|---|---|---|
| Personal consumption expenditure | 945 | Income of employees | 800 |
| Sales to other domestic firms | 115[1] | Rent | 10 |
| Government current expenditure | 300 | Purchases from other domestic firms | 220[1] |
| Gross domestic capital formation: | | Gross trading profit, including stock appreciation and before deducting depreciation, transferred to appropriation account | **520** |
| Fixed capital formation | 150 | | |
| Value of physical increase in stock and work in progress—[15+17] | **−32** | | 1,550 |
| | | *less* Stock appreciation | **−17** |
| Exports of goods and services | 445 | | |
| *less* Imports of goods and services | −80 | | |
| | 1,843 | | |
| *less* Taxes on expenditure | −350 | | |
| Subsidies | 40 | | |
| | 1,533 | | 1,533 |

*Appropriation account of X Ltd*

| | £000 | | £000 |
|---|---|---|---|
| Gross trading profit transferred from production account | **520** | Interest | 25 |
| | | Dividends (after adding back tax) [105+86] | **191** |
| | | Undistributed income before tax | **304** |
| | 520 | | 520 |
| Undistributed income before tax | **304** | Provision for direct taxation (after deducting tax on dividends) [310−86] | **224** |
| | | Undistributed income after provision for tax, including stock appreciation, and before deducting depreciation | 80 |
| | 304 | | 304 |

[1] These items disappear by cancellation when merged in the national accounts.

The rearrangement of the contents of the accounts calls for some comment. In the production account the removal of the value of physical stock appreciation to the left-hand side allows it to be linked with the gross increase in fixed capital. The two items together give (in the national aggregation) gross domestic investment (capital formation). The removal of imports to the left-hand side similarly allows them to be linked with exports to give net investment abroad. The difference between these two items in the national accounts represents an increase in the value of net claims held against the rest of the world (possibly in the form of a decrease in liabilities to the rest of the world), or in gold, as we see from *X Ltd*'s asset-liability accounts in which the excess of exports over imports reflects a fall in claims of non-residents against the company and a transfer of money from them to the company. In the national accounts the aggregate of investment abroad, together with gross domestic investment, gives total gross investment or capital formation attributable to the activities recorded in the production account.

There is a further reason, however, for listing imports and stock changes on the left-hand side of the account: thereby the figure of £1,843,000 given as the sub-total, less the £115,000 sales to other firms which will cancel out in the aggregation, reflects *X Ltd*'s part of the 'gross national product at market prices'. This total represents the value of production before deducting purchase taxes or adding subsidies. These are both brought over to this side of the account so that the national account may also record gross national product at factor cost. This magnitude is also given in the aggregation by the total of the right-hand side of all the separate production accounts, after cancelling the purchases from other firms and deducting stock appreciation. The latter, as it is not regarded as part of national product, is deducted on both sides (on the left-hand side by increasing, in *X Ltd*'s case, the negative stock change).

Businesses may, of course, in addition to receiving payment for goods and services supplied, receive interest on holdings of the national debt, representing transfers of money from the government, which are not normally classified as payments for a factor of production. These are not, therefore, entered in the production account, but are allocated to the appropriation section, and will swell interest or dividends paid, or undistributed income, correspondingly.

If *X Ltd* had been, not a company, but a public corporation with financial independence (as distinct from a government trading department) the accounting would have been substantially the same, though there would have been no dividends paid. On the other hand, government trading departments without financial independence would have been treated (in the United Kingdom accounts) very like private non-corporate businesses except that their profits would have been regarded as part of *government*, and not *household*, income, and classified accordingly.

We have now, so to speak, examined under a microscope sections from those parts of the national income accounts which are concerned with the activities of persons and businesses and seen how the national income aggregates and figures are related to those of fairly typical individual units. In particular we have seen how the accounts are, in essence, no more than summaries of movements of claims and goods and of some changes in the values of goods, even though they are complicated by the fact that some of these 'movements' are only conceptual and do not correspond to real life transactions, though they may reflect book-keeping entries made by transactors. (An example of this is the accounting transfer of gross trading profit from production account to appropriation account, which, in actual firms, may be represented by a book entry, but will not reflect any transfer of ownership of claims.)

We could proceed to examine the government sector in the same way as we have done the other parts of the economy, showing, for example, how the non-trading activities of the various central government departments and agencies, and local governments, fit into the framework of the national accounts. We think, however, that as the connexion between detail and aggregate has now been demonstrated the best use for the remaining space is to investigate the relation between a complete system of national income accounts and the complex of movements in claims and goods which it reflects. In this way it may be made easier for the reader to grasp the essential nature of the system of national income accounts as a whole. Before we pass on to this task in Chapter 10, however, we show in the Appendix to this chapter how the simple system of accounts of Chapter 3 may be rearranged in the form more familiar to readers of the official statistics. This follows naturally from our discussion in this chapter.

## APPENDIX TO CHAPTER 9

In this appendix we intend to develop the simple set of national income accounts of Chapters 3 and 4 into a form approximating more closely to that used in the United Kingdom National Income Blue Books. Readers should note, however, that we shall deliberately refrain from increasing the complexity of the accounts by introducing all the detail which appears in the official published statistics. We are concerned not with providing a detailed guide to the latter but rather with suggesting a method of approach to their use and interpretation. Readers who refer to the latest Blue Book issued at the time of writing—*National Income and Expenditure 1966* (H.M. Stationery Office, August 1966)—will find that we have arranged the figures in a way that corresponds, so far as the simplified data allow, to the presentation of the main summary tables in that publication.

Our first step is to restate the set of accounts which appeared in Chapter 3, section 3. This will give us the opportunity, first, to make some preliminary rearrangements which will simplify the transition to the new form, and, secondly, to make some additional assumptions and insert an additional transaction in order to illustrate points not dealt with in the original set.

We consider first the firms account as it appears on page 50. We shall assume that of the sum of 90 shown in the account as paid by firms for factor services, 14 is interest and dividends paid out by corporate business, leaving 76 paid for other factors of production employed by corporate business and for all factors of non-corporate business. Gross domestic investment, 10, we shall divide into gross fixed capital formation, 8, and value of the physical increase in stocks, 2, with zero stock appreciation.

The only alteration we shall make in the households account results from one of those made to firms account: the 14 we have allocated to corporate interest and dividends will now be shown separately.

We shall make the very simplified government account of Chapter 3 slightly more realistic by assuming that a current grant of 2 has been made to an overseas government by the home government, which will decrease government saving by the same amount since we shall not assume any corresponding rise in other government spending. (As explained in Chapter 3, grants abroad are not, in the United Kingdom, put through firms account like income paid abroad —they are not regarded as part of gross national product.) A corresponding adjustment must be made in the rest of the world account.

The above change will produce a consequential change in the capital account: government saving falls from 3 to 1, as does net lending to, or increase in borrowing from, the rest of the world.

Our amended accounts are as follows:

*Firms*

| | | | | | |
|---|---|---|---|---|---|
| Sales of consumption goods and services to households | | 85 | Purchases of factor services from households: | | |
| Sales of current goods and services to government | | 15 | Interest and dividends paid by corporate business | 14 | |
| Gross domestic investment: | | | Other incomes | 76 | 90 |
| Fixed capital formation | 8 | | Direct taxes on corporate business | | 4 |
| Value of physical increase in stocks and work in progress | 2 | 10 | Indirect taxes | | 13 |
| Sales of exports to non-residents | | 10 | Firms' saving (corporate business) | | 6 |
| *less* purchases of imports from non-residents | | −7 | | | |
| | | 113 | | | 113 |

*Households*

| | | | | |
|---|---|---|---|---|
| Sales of factor services to firms: | | | Purchases of consumption goods and services from firms | 85 |
| Interest and dividends from corporate business | 14 | | Direct taxes | 6 |
| Other incomes | 76 | 90 | Households' saving | 4 |
| Transfer payments from government | | 5 | | |
| | | 95 | | 95 |

*Government*

| | | | |
|---|---|---|---|
| Direct taxes | 10 | Purchases of current goods and services from firms | 15 |
| Indirect taxes | 13 | Transfers to households | 5 |
| | | Current grant to overseas government | 2 |
| | | Government saving | 1 |
| | 23 | | 23 |

*Rest of the world*

| | | | |
|---|---|---|---|
| Sales of imports to firms | 7 | Purchases of exports from firms | 10 |
| Grant to overseas government | 2 | | |
| Net investment abroad | 1 | | |
| | 10 | | 10 |

*Capital account*

| | | | | |
|---|---|---|---|---|
| Firms' saving | 6 | Gross domestic investment: | | |
| Households' saving | 4 | Fixed capital formation | 8 | |
| Government saving | 1 | Value of physical increase in stocks and work in progress | 2 | 10 |
| | | Net investment abroad | | 1 |
| | 11 | | | 11 |

We can now rearrange our accounts in 'Blue Book form' in the way already indicated earlier in this chapter. Firms account we split into production and corporate income appropriation accounts. We then have:

*Production account (showing gross national product)*

| | | | |
|---|---|---|---|
| Consumers' expenditure | 85 | Income of employees, Forces, self-employed persons, rent | 76 |
| Government current expenditure | 15 | Gross trading profits of companies and public corporations [14+4+6] | 24 |
| Gross domestic capital formation: | | | |
| Fixed capital formation | 8 | | |
| Value of physical increase in stocks and work in progress | 2 | | |
| Exports (including all income from abroad) | 10 | | |
| *less* Imports (including all income paid abroad) | −7 | | |
| Gross national expenditure at market prices | 113 | | |
| *less* Taxes on expenditure less subsidies | −13 | | |
| Gross national expenditure at factor cost | 100 | National income and depreciation | 100 |

The appropriation account is:

*Corporate income appropriation account*

| | | | |
|---|---|---|---|
| Gross trading profits of companies and trading surpluses of public corporations | 24 | Interest and dividends paid to persons | 14 |
| | | Undistributed income before tax | 10 |
| | 24 | | 24 |
| Undistributed income before tax | 10 | Provisions for direct taxation | 4 |
| | | Undistributed income after tax, before deducting provisions for depreciation (corporate saving) | 6 |
| | 10 | | 10 |

Households' account becomes:

*Personal income and expenditure*

| | | | |
|---|---|---|---|
| Income of employees, members of the Forces and self-employed persons, rent | 76 | Consumers' expenditure | 85 |
| Interest and dividends | 14 | Provision for taxes on income | 6 |
| Interest on national debt, national insurance benefits and other current grants from government | 5 | Saving, before deducting provisions for depreciation of business capital equipment of self-employed persons | 4 |
| | 95 | | 95 |

The government account we shall split into two accounts, one for central government and one for local government, assigning to each account its appropriate receipts and payments. We shall assume: (*a*) that of the indirect taxes of 13 received by government, 2 are local rates; (*b*) that of purchases of current goods and services by government, 3 are made by local authorities; and (*c*) that local authorities had neither saving nor dissaving. When we draft the new accounts on that basis we find that this will leave us with a gap, in both accounts, but on opposite sides, of 1. This, we assume, is the amount of the current annual grant by central government to local authorities. We then have:

*Revenue account of central government*

| | | | |
|---|---|---|---|
| Taxes on income | 10 | Current expenditure on goods and services [15−3] | 12 |
| Taxes on expenditure [13−2] | 11 | National debt interest, national insurance benefits and other grants to persons | 5 |
| | | Current grants to local authorities | 1 |
| | | Current grant to overseas government | 2 |
| | | Surplus (saving) | 1 |
| | 21 | | 21 |

*Current account of local authorities*

| | | | |
|---|---|---|---|
| Rates | 2 | Current expenditure on goods and services | 3 |
| Current grants from central government | 1 | Surplus (saving) | 0 |
| | 3 | | 3 |

The account for the rest of the world shows there has been a net acquisition of gold or claims on non-residents (or reduction in claims by non-residents). Apart from the wording, the account appears very much as in our earlier presentation:

*Transactions with the rest of the world*

| | | | |
|---|---|---|---|
| Receipts by rest of the world for imports of goods and services from, and income paid to, abroad | 7 | Payments by rest of the world for exports of goods and services to, and income received from, abroad | 10 |
| Current grant to overseas government | 2 | | |
| Net investment abroad (increase in claims on rest of the world or gold holding, or decrease in rest of the world's claims on domestic economy) | 1 | | |
| | 10 | | 10 |

Apart from rather more elaborate wording the combined capital account is also much as it appeared in the earlier presentation. It is worth noting, however, that had any of the right-hand items been negative they would still have been retained on that side of the account (as negative items) in order that both sides should sum to the magnitude defined as total savings or investment. We have:

*Combined capital account*

| | | | |
|---|---|---|---|
| Saving, before deducting provisions for depreciation: | | Gross fixed capital formation | 8 |
| Persons | 4 | Value of physical increase in stocks and work in progress | 2 |
| Companies and public corporations | 6 | Investment abroad (net) | 1 |
| Central government surplus on revenue account | 1 | | |
| Total saving | 11 | Total investment | 11 |

Had there been any stock appreciation element in savings and investment this would have been eliminated on both sides.

We shall end this appendix by commenting on so-called 'taxes on capital' already mentioned briefly in Chapter 3. In the United Kingdom national income accounts the amounts of such taxes are indicated by including them as a receipt in the central government account, which shows a correspondingly higher surplus. As they are not, however, recorded as payments in the personal income and expenditure account, the surplus of which is, therefore, not reduced, the savings of the central government have to be shown in the capital account net of the capital taxes, that is at a lower figure than the surplus shown in the central government account; if they were not, the capital account would not balance. In other words, persons and not government are credited with the savings from which taxes on capital are assumed to be paid and the government account includes a 'memorandum' receipt which is not matched by a payment elsewhere in the accounts.

# 10

# ASSET STRUCTURE ANALYSIS

## 1. *Introduction*

We have now come to the last stage in our journey. In this chapter we shall pursue further our examination of the changes in asset structure of the various sectors of the economy which underlie conventional national income statistics. We hope thereby to show students more clearly the relation between those statistics and the complex and continual shuffling and reshuffling of assets and liabilities that comprise economic activity.

Changes in the kind of assets and liabilities held by different groups of people and organisations are of considerable significance to the economist: they may throw light on important trends within the economy and on the probable future behaviour of members of these groups. It is, for example, of great interest to know whether or not businesses as a whole have been increasing or decreasing their money holdings: this may be relevant to government monetary or fiscal policy. If money holdings have changed it is important to know why. Has there been a corresponding change (investment or dis-investment) in business stocks? Has business as a whole been borrowing or lending, and if so, from whom or to whom? This will be indicated by changes in the claims on business of persons, government, financial institutions, or non-residents. A change in the level of stocks suggests the question 'has it been voluntary or involuntary?' Thus, a rise might indicate growing slackness of trade and inability to sell goods—perhaps because wage rises had forced up costs or because overseas demand had fallen; or, on the other hand, it might indicate that banks were lending more freely, thus allowing businesses to increase stocks, perhaps in expectation of the price rises that were thereby being engendered, drawing in more imports from the rest of the world, and possibly making exports harder to sell.

This kind of consideration suggests that if we are to have an adequate picture of the economy we need a more detailed analysis of the asset changes of each sector than are given by conventional national income accounts. It is true that, at present, the statistics available in most, if not all, countries are probably inadequate to provide as detailed a picture as many people would like. On the other hand, a good many statistics of changes in the assets and liabilities of different groups of transactors are published and are studied by those interested in the state of the economy. These statistics are not usually presented, however, in the form of a complete system, related to the national income accounts, and it will, perhaps, be useful to examine the framework of such a system.

### 2. *The analysis of asset structure by sectors*

Our plan is to expand the simplified national income accounts set set out in the Appendix to Chapter 9 into a more complex (though still highly simplified) set of accounts in which the asset structure changes underlying the original set can be analysed and classified. We shall, because it is simpler, use the form of accounts discussed in Part I of the book, and as given at the beginning of the Appendix to Chapter 9 and not the modified form given in the latter part of the Appendix, except that it will be convenient again to show imports as a payment in the firms account rather than as a negative receipt. The corporate income appropriation account will thus be merged into firms account, and central and local government will be combined in one account. (The figures in our accounts will, therefore, differ from the accounts of Chapter 3 only to the extent that they will include the additions and amendments described at the beginning of the Appendix to Chapter 9 and an account of the revised treatment of imports.)

The accounts will be divided into five sectors: 'firms', 'households', 'government', 'financial institutions' and 'banks'. Readers are already familiar with the first three sectors, but some further explanation is needed with respect to 'financial institutions' and 'banks' which are really sub-divisions of the firms sector.

The reasons for introducing these additional sectors are as follows. In the first place, changes in the quantity of money—which, in modern economies, means bank deposits and notes—take place through an alteration in the structure of bank assets and liabilities.

Note-issuing and deposit banks are, indeed, peculiar among institutions, in that their liabilities *are* money. It is thus necessary to introduce banks into our picture since they provide the link between changes in the quantity of money and the other events of the economy.

Secondly, it is among the liabilities and (in some countries) the assets of banks that we find an important part of the debts due to, or from, the rest of the world. Changes in these are of great importance to any country with much international trade, and are among the more significant indicators used in economic forecasting. Such data can, of course, be published separately, but by integrating them into our accounts we can get a clearer picture of how changes in these balances are related to the economic events of the rest of the economy.

Thirdly, it is not possible to have a clear idea of the events which underlie savings-investment and liquidity concepts without an appreciation of the lending and borrowing functions of banks and other financial institutions.

Hence our category 'banks' will be assumed to cover the deposit-banking and note-issuing institutions; 'financial institutions' will cover other institutions whose main activities consist of raising money on the one hand and re-lending or otherwise 'placing' it on the other. Our classification is necessarily simplified and we ignore such complications as the relation between deposit banks and the central bank. For a practical system it would almost certainly be desirable to provide separate sectors for the central bank and the other banks. We have kept our scheme as simple as reasonably possible by assuming that there is no separate central bank. We also assume that all money transactions take the form of bank deposit transfers. (Accounting for bank notes, which are, of course, liabilities of banks, is essentially the same.)

We have, for the sake of simplicity, ignored interest and dividend payments, payments to factors of production, and payments for services, made to or by financial institutions and banks.

For each sector we shall first set out the national income account as already given in the Appendix to Chapter 9. Beneath each of these income accounts we shall give asset-liability accounts for the same sector, recording the net changes in the sector's holdings of goods and claims for the period, with an account for each class of asset or liability. (We shall, for the purpose of our arithmetic, have to select arbitrary figures for the various changes in asset structure from which the income accounts are derived.) It follows necessarily that in each sector the sum of the changes recorded in the asset-liability accounts will be equal to the net change in the income account, for the latter is merely an analysis of certain of those changes by types of transaction. We emphasise this by printing the income accounts in bold type. The net change recorded in each income account, equal to the sum of the changes in asset-liability accounts, will be, by definition, the net saving or dissaving of the sector for the period. We shall be able, by examining the changes in asset structure shown in the accounts, to appreciate, if we have not already done so, the derivation and implications of the investment and savings totals in national income accounts and to see from another aspect the role of the accounts for 'capital' and 'rest of the world'.

This set of accounts thus provides the framework for a summary of economic events wider in scope than is given in the national income accounts which, however, fit into, and form part of, our more comprehensive set.

The conventions used in these accounts are the same as those already discussed in Chapter 9 in connexion with the accounts of *A* and *X Ltd.* The derivation of the income accounts from the asset-liability accounts is indicated by printing in bold type not only the income accounts themselves, but those items in the other accounts from which the income accounts are constructed. All other items represent asset structure changes which do not enter into the income flow calculations, and which have been arbitrarily chosen for demonstration purposes. The few items recorded here symbolise, of course, a vast class of such changes in real life: we have not attempted to do more than sketch in a few transactions in order to illustrate the general principles.

The reader should remember when he examines the accounts that they do not purport to record *all* the transactions that have taken place during the period, even in aggregate. They record *net changes* over the year in such detail as is considered useful and can be included without making them too cumbrous. For example, in the accounts of firms, we have shown sales of consumers' goods by firms to households, 85 in total, settled as to 83 in money and as to 2 in increased debts due to households to firms (of which we assume debts to the value of 1 are then sold by firms to banks). In fact, of course, a much greater proportion of sales might, in the first place, have been made on credit terms—that is, in exchange for debts of households which later would have been converted into money when the customers paid in the ordinary course of business. Nor do the accounts as we have them disclose the absolute level of consumer debt. The account recording debts due from consumers to firms only states the *increase* in debts over the year. The ideal accounts would no doubt record the day-by-day flow of debts, money and goods. Our coarser treatment here must be attributed partly to the limitations of space and partly to recognition of the fact that, as we said earlier, all classification implies some departure from precision: how much inaccuracy is accepted in actual statistical work must depend on guesses about the gains that would result and the sacrifices that would have to be incurred with greater attention to detail.

We may, however, take this opportunity of noting that the absolute size of holdings of goods, other assets and liabilities by all sectors of the economy is of considerable importance for the applied economist. The lack of adequate classified data of these holdings is one of the serious gaps in current economic statistics. Although we have not introduced figures into the accounts representative of the total size of debts and liabilities and of holdings of goods (as distinct from changes) this could very easily be done, either by adding opening balances to the accounts and allowing the closing balances to record changes during the year plus opening balances, or by providing some kind of balance sheet for each sector summarising asset and liability holdings. (Many of the figures would not be available in practice, but some would. It would be worth while making a start.)

We now turn to the accounts. The reader should bear in mind that in each sector for every entry in the asset-liability accounts there must be a corresponding entry elsewhere in that sector, either in the income account (if the first entry is a component of the net change in wealth of that sector), in which case both entries will be on the same side of the respective accounts; or in one of the other asset or liability accounts (if the first entry merely represents one aspect of a change in asset structure), in which case the entries will be on opposite sides of the accounts concerned. All income account items reflect a corresponding item or items on the same side of one or more asset-liability accounts. Furthermore, any rearrangement of assets in one sector and any acquisition or loss of assets, except where the change is the production of new goods, or the use of stocks, or the acquisition or loss of overseas assets or liabilities, must be reflected by corresponding changes in another sector. It is worth while tracing through these correspondences. In the income accounts, saving is shown as an excess of receipts over payments and not as a payment to capital account.

The 'build-up' of the income accounts from the asset-liability accounts is indicated by figures in square brackets.

## (I) FIRMS[1]

**Income account of firms**

| | | | | | |
|---|---|---|---|---|---|
| **1=10 +24** | **Sales of consumption goods and services to households [83+2]** | **85** | **5=16 +34** | **Purchases of factor services from households (including interest and dividend payments) [79+11]** | **90** |
| **2=11** | **Sales of current goods and services to government** | **15** | **6=17** | **Purchases of imports from non-residents** | **7** |
| **3=27 +28** | **Gross domestic investment [8+2]** | **10** | **7=18** | **Direct taxes** | **4** |
| **4=12 +30** | **Sales of exports to non-residents [8+2]** | **10** | **8=19** | **Indirect taxes** | **13** |
| | | **120** | | | **114** |
| **9** | **Net change = corporate saving** | **6** | | | |

*Money (bank deposits) held by firms*

| | *Receipts* | | | *Payments* | |
|---|---|---|---|---|---|
| 10 (see 1) | Sales of consumption goods and services to households | 83 | 16 (see 5) | Purchases of factor services from households (including interest and dividend payments) | 79 |
| 11=2 | Sales of current goods and services to government | 15 | 17=6 | Purchases of imports from non-residents | 7 |
| 12 (see 4) | Sales of exports to non-residents | 8 | 18=7 | Direct taxes paid to government | 4 |
| 13=36 | Issues of debenture loans to financial institutions | 1 | 19=8 | Indirect taxes paid to government | 13 |
| 14=25 | Sales to banks of debts of households | 1 | 20 (see 38) | Purchases from banks of government securities | 2 |
| 15=31 +32 | Sales to banks of bills of non-residents | 5 | 21 (see 38) | Purchases from households of government securities | 1 |
| | | | 22 (see 38) | Purchases from government of government securities | 2 |
| | | 113 | | | 108 |
| 23 | Net change = rise in firms' holdings of bank deposits | 5 | | | |

[1] Excluding banks and financial institutions.

This account shows that though firms' savings (see the income account) were 6, their bank deposits have risen only by 5. This is because (*a*), as will be shown by the other accounts, not all the flows shown in the income account were of money, and (*b*) there have been exchanges of assets and liabilities for money merely representing changes in the form in which wealth is held.

*Debts of households to firms*

| | *Increase in debt* | | | *Decrease in debt* | |
|---|---|---|---|---|---|
| 24 (see 1) | Sales of consumption goods and services to households | 2 | 25=14 | Sales of debts to banks | 1 |
| | | 2 | | | 1 |
| 26 | Net change=rise in trade debts due to firms | 1 | | | |

This account records 'consumer credit' and includes amounts owing by households for goods supplied on instalment credit. The sale of debt to banks represents the transfer by firms of some of this financing to banks. Had the debt been taken over by hire-purchase finance companies a sale to financial institutions would have been recorded.

*Goods owned by firms*

| | *Increases* | | | *Decreases* | |
|---|---|---|---|---|---|
| 27 (see 3) | Fixed capital equipment | 8 | | | |
| 28 (see 3) | Value of physical rise in stocks and work in progress | 2 | | | |
| | | 10 | | | — |
| 29 | Net change=gross domestic capital formation | 10 | | | |

This account records the rise, resulting from productive activity or purchase overseas, in capital equipment, stocks and work in progress before deduction of depreciation, using the conventional valuations as discussed in Chapter 4. We have assumed stock appreciation is zero. Had it been positive or negative it could have been eliminated in this account and in the income account or shown separately in each, as desired.

*Bills of exchange given by non-residents to firms*

| | *Increases* | | | *Decreases* | |
|---|---|---|---|---|---|
| 30 (see 4) | Sales of exports to non-residents | 2 | 31 (see 15) | Bills held at beginning of year sold to banks | 3 |
| | | | 32 (see 15) | Bills received during year sold to banks | 2 |
| | | 2 | | | 5 |
| | | | 33 | Net change = fall in firms' holdings of non-residents' bills | 3 |

Here firms have received bills of exchange for some of their exports. Firms have discounted the bills they received this year and also bills outstanding at the end of last year.

*Equity of households in firms ('liability' of non-corporate firms to their owners)*

| | *Decrease in equity* | | | *Increase in equity* | |
|---|---|---|---|---|---|
| | | | 34 (see 5) | Gross trading profits not withdrawn from businesses by households | 11 |
| | | — | | | 11 |
| | | | 35 | Net change = rise in equity interests of households in non-corporate business | 11 |

The profits of non-corporate business are treated as part of factor incomes of households: this account records the part not transferred in money. As explained in Chapter 9, corporate saving could be, but is not usually, recorded in this way.

*Liability of corporate businesses to debenture holders*

| | *Decrease in liability* | | | *Increase in liability* | |
|---|---|---|---|---|---|
| | | | 36 = 13 | Securities issued to financial institutions | 1 |
| | | — | | | 1 |
| | | | 37 | Net change = rise in fixed-return interests of financial institutions in corporate business | 1 |

Businesses can change their money holdings by buying or selling their own securities, as here, or by buying or selling those of other sectors they already hold, as below.

*Government securities owned by firms*

| | *Increase* | | *Decrease* |
|---|---|---|---|
| 38 = 20 +21 +22 | Purchase from households, government and banks | 5 | |
| | | 5 | — |
| 39 | Net change = rise in holdings of business sector | 5 | |

If we now summarise all the net changes in the above accounts we have:

*Income account*

| | | |
|---|---|---|
| 9. | Net increase in wealth = saving | 6 |

*Asset-liability accounts*

| | | | |
|---|---|---|---|
| Increases in Assets | | | |
| 23. | Money | | 5 |
| 26. | Debts of households | | 1 |
| 29. | Goods | | 10 |
| 39. | Government securities | | 5 |
| | | | 21 |
| *less* decreases in assets/increases in liabilities | | | |
| 33. | Bills of exchange of non-residents | 3 | |
| 35. | Equity interests in non-corporate business | 11 | |
| 37. | Debenture securities | 1 | 15 |
| | Net increase in wealth | | 6 |

## (II) HOUSEHOLDS

**Income account of households**

| | | | | | |
|---|---|---|---|---|---|
| **40=45 +58** | **Sales of factor services to firms [79+11]** | **90** | **42=48 +54** | **Purchases of consumption goods and services from firms [83+2]** | **85** |
| **41=46** | **Transfer payments from government** | **5** | **43=50** | **Direct taxes** | **6** |
| | | **95** | | | **91** |
| **44** | **Net change=saving** | **4** | | | |

*Money (bank deposits) held by households*

| | *Receipts* | | | *Payments* | |
|---|---|---|---|---|---|
| 45 (see 40) | Sales of factor services to firms | 79 | 48 (see 42) | Purchases of consumption goods and services from firms | 83 |
| 46 =41 | Transfer payments from government | 5 | 49=56 | Repayments to banks of debts for consumption goods | 1 |
| 47=62 | Sales of government securities to firms | 1 | 50=43 | Direct taxes | 6 |
| 47a =61a | Receipts under life assurance policies | 1 | 51=60 | Premiums paid to life assurance offices | 2 |
| | | 86 | | | 92 |
| | | | 52 | Net change=fall in households' holdings of bank deposits | 6 |

*Liabilities of households to firms*

| | *Decrease in liabilities* | | | *Increase in liabilities* | |
|---|---|---|---|---|---|
| 53=57 | Liabilities taken over by banks | 1 | 54 (see 42) | Liabilities incurred with firms for consumption goods | 2 |
| | | 1 | | | 2 |
| | | | 55 | Net change=rise in liabilities of households | 1 |

Households' liabilities to firms fall when these are taken over by banks, their liabilities to banks rising correspondingly (see item 57).

*Liabilities of households to banks*

| *Decrease in liabilities* | | | *Increase in liabilities* | | |
|---|---|---|---|---|---|
| 56=49 | Liabilities settled by money payment to banks | 1 | 57=53 | Liabilities taken over from firms | 1 |
| | | 1 | | | 1 |

Households have reimbursed banks, thus restoring to them the funds they advanced to firms when they took over the debt.

*Equity interests in non-corporate firms owned by households*

| *Increases* | | | *Decreases* | | |
|---|---|---|---|---|---|
| 58 (see 40) | Gross trading profits left in businesses | 11 | | | |
| | | 11 | | | — |
| 59 | Net change = rise in value of equity interests | 11 | | | |

*Life assurance policies, etc.*

| *Increases* | | | *Decreases* | | |
|---|---|---|---|---|---|
| 60=51 | Premiums | 2 | 61a=47a | Claims | 1 |
| | | 2 | | | 1 |
| 61 | Net change = rise in interest of households in the funds of life assurance offices | 1 | | | |

*Government securities owned by households*

| *Increases* | | | *Decreases* | | |
|---|---|---|---|---|---|
| | | | 62=47 | Sales to firms | 1 |
| | | — | | | 1 |
| | | | 63 | Net change = fall in holdings of securities | 1 |

Summarising the changes in households' wealth and individual assets we have:

*Income account*

| | | |
|---|---|---|
| 44. Net increase in wealth = saving | | 4 |

*Asset-liability accounts*

| | | |
|---|---|---|
| Increases in assets | | |
| 59. Equity interests in firms | | 11 |
| 61. Life assurance policies | | 1 |
| | | 12 |
| *less* decreases in assets/increases in liabilities | | |
| 52. Money | 6 | |
| 55. Liabilities to firms | 1 | |
| 63. Government securities | 1 | 8 |
| Net increase in wealth | | 4 |

## (III) GOVERNMENT

**Income account of government**

| | | | | | |
|---|---|---|---|---|---|
| **64=70 +71** | **Direct taxes [4+6]** | **10** | **66=74** | **Purchases of current goods and services from firms** | **15** |
| **65=72** | **Indirect taxes** | **13** | **67=75** | **Transfers to households** | **5** |
| | | | **68=80** | **Grant to overseas government** | **2** |
| | | **23** | | | **22** |
| **69** | **Net change = government saving** | **1** | | | |

*Money (bank deposits) held by government*

| *Receipts* | | | *Payments* | | |
|---|---|---|---|---|---|
| 70 (see 64) | Direct taxes from firms | 4 | 74=66 | Purchases of current goods and services from firms | 15 |
| 71 (see 64) | Direct taxes from households | 6 | 75=67 | Transfers to households | 5 |
| 72=65 | Indirect taxes from firms | 13 | 76=77 | Purchase of government securities from banks | 5 |
| 73=78 | Government securities sold to firms | 2 | | | |
| | | 25 | | | 25 |

The items in bold type in this account, the government's cash account, reflect the outcome of the annual financial budget.

In the United Kingdom the government holdings of bank deposits do not vary greatly. If the government finds itself with an increased balance at the Bank of England it will use this to repay government debt. Item 76 might represent this kind of transaction.

Note that by levying taxes the government can obtain bank deposits which it can then, if it wishes, re-transfer to firms or households, either directly, by buying government securities from them, or indirectly, by buying government securities from banks, leaving banks to re-expand their assets (and deposits) by lending to firms or households. This is the process by which government may be able to increase national saving: but this will only happen if the increased taxation reduces *consumption.*

*National Debt (liability of government to holders of government securities, etc.)*

| | *Decrease in debt* | | | *Increase in debt* | |
|---|---|---|---|---|---|
| 77=76 | Purchase of securities from banks | 5 | 78=73 | Sale of securities to firms | 2 |
| | | 5 | | | 2 |
| 79 | Net change=fall in national debt | 3 | | | |

Item 78 might represent subscriptions by business firms to new issues of government bonds.

We have here assumed that national debt changes have been related only to holdings of national debt by residents. A more complete scheme might have shown also changes in *non-residents'* holdings. These would require a separate account, for, not being changes in *domestic* claims, they would form part of national investment or disinvestment for the period, and would have generally a different significance from changes in residents' holdings.

*Government holdings of gold and overseas currencies*

| | *Increases* | | | *Decreases* | |
|---|---|---|---|---|---|
| | | | 80=68 | Payment to overseas government, by way of grant | 2 |
| | | — | | | 2 |
| | | | 81 | Net change=fall in exchange reserves | 2 |

The above account represents what, in the United Kingdom, is called the exchange equalisation account. In this set of accounts we have assumed that all external transactions, except the grant shown here, are settled by changes in non-residents' holdings of bank deposits (see below). In fact, many would be settled in gold or dollars, etc. The government would then sell (or buy) gold or dollars to (or from) firms and thereby gain or lose bank deposits. Thus a rise in imports from the USA would cause government gold or dollar holdings to fall and government bank deposits to rise as dollars were sold to firms to pay for these.

We may summarise the government sector changes as follows:

*Income account*

| | |
|---|---|
| 69. Net increase in wealth = saving | 1 |

*Asset-liability accounts*

| | |
|---|---|
| Increase in assets/decrease in liabilities | |
| 81. Gold and overseas currencies | −2 |
| 79. National debt | 3 |
| Net increase in wealth | 1 |

## (IV) FINANCIAL INSTITUTIONS[1]

As indicated on page 175 we have ignored expenses and profits of these institutions. Hence there is no income account. A more serious omission is the absence of any receipt of interest or dividends. Had these been included, money receipts would have been higher and a corresponding rise would have been recorded in the life office funds account. There would have been corresponding changes in other sectors.

[1] We have confined our types of financial institution to one: life assurance offices. Readers should be able to fit building societies and other institutions into this pattern for themselves.

*Money (bank deposits)*

| | *Receipts* | | | *Payments* | |
|---|---|---|---|---|---|
| 82=86 | Premiums received by life assurance offices from households | 2 | 83=85 | Claims paid to households | 1 |
| | | | 84=88 | Debenture securities purchased by life offices | 1 |
| | | 2 | | | 2 |

*Life office funds*

| | *Decreases* | | | *Increases* | |
|---|---|---|---|---|---|
| 85=83 | Claims paid in money | 1 | 86=82 | Money premiums received | 2 |
| | | 1 | | | 2 |
| | | | 87 | Net change=rise in life office funds | 1 |

The net increase here represents the rise in the 'claim' of households on life funds in respect of their policies—see item 61. Item 88 shows the corresponding rise in investments.

*Debenture securities of corporate business held by life offices*

| | *Increase* | | *Decrease* |
|---|---|---|---|
| 88=84 | Purchased for money | 1 | |
| | | 1 | — |
| 89 | Net change=rise in investments of life funds | 1 | |

For simplicity we have allowed this single account to symbolise the many purchases and sales of securities and other property by life offices and other financial institutions.

The summary of the financial institutions sector is as follows:

*Asset-liability accounts*

| | |
|---|---|
| Increase in assets | |
| 89. Debentures of corporate business | 1 |
| *less* increase in liabilities | |
| 87. Life funds | 1 |
| Net change | 0 |

### (v) BANKS

As with financial institutions we have ignored all income account transactions of banks. In fact, of course, there would be receipts and payments of interest and dividends on both sides of the money account, receipts of commissions, etc., and payments of expenses, the net difference being the saving of banks.

*Domestic deposits (liabilities of banks to residents)*

| | *Decreases* | | | *Increases* | |
|---|---|---|---|---|---|
| 90 | Deposits transferred by: | | 91 | Deposits acquired by: | |
| | Firms | 108 | | Firms | 113 |
| | Households | 92 | | Households | 86 |
| | Government | 25 | | Government | 25 |
| | Financial institutions | 2 | | Financial institutions | 2 |
| | | 227 | | | 226 |
| 92 | Net change = fall in domestic deposits | 1 | | | |

All the detailed money receipts and payments of the other sectors, except receipts from, and payments to, non-residents, shown in the next account, are summarised in the two sides of this account. Most of these receipts and payments are simply transfers from one domestic bank customer to another. The remainder result from changes in bank assets and other liabilities and are shown below. As the receipts and payments are here summarised in aggregate it is not possible to relate the individual changes in each account in this sector to one another.

*Deposits of non-residents (liabilities of banks to rest of the world)*

| | *Decreases* | | | *Increases* | |
|---|---|---|---|---|---|
| 93 | Deposits transferred by non-residents to firms in payment for exports (see 91) | 8 | 95 | Deposits transferred to non-residents from firms in payment for imports (see 90) | 7 |
| 94 =103 | Decrease in deposits in respect of bills of non-residents paid in due course | 5 | | | |
| | | 13 | | | 7 |
| 96 | Net change = fall in non-residents' deposits | 6 | | | |

*Government securities held by banks*

| | | | Decreases | |
|---|---|---|---|---|
| | | 97 | Sales to firms (see 90) | 2 |
| | | 98 | Sales to government (see 90) | 5 |
| | — | | | 7 |
| | | 99 | Net change = fall in holding of securities | 7 |

*Debts of households to banks*

| | Increases | | | Decreases | |
|---|---|---|---|---|---|
| 100 | Purchased from firms (see 91) | 1 | 101 | Repaid by households (see 90) | 1 |

*Bills of exchange payable by non-residents*

| | Increases | | | Decreases | |
|---|---|---|---|---|---|
| 102 | Purchased from firms (see 91) | 5 | 103 =94 | Repaid by non-residents | 5 |

The transfers of deposits between sectors and from residents to non-residents cannot affect the total of bank deposits. Net changes in the assets of banks—for example in government securities—must do so, however, for the corresponding payment of money to, or receipt from, banks as a whole *means* the reduction, or increase, of bank deposits that is *a change in the quantity of money*.

Bank balance sheets do not normally distinguish between deposits of residents and non-residents. The distinction is, however, of vital importance, for the former represent merely claims of the nation as a whole on its own resources, while the latter represent claims of the rest of the world on those resources.

The summary of the banks sector is as follows:

*Asset-liability accounts*

| | |
|---|---|
| Decreases in liabilities | |
| 92. Domestic deposits | 1 |
| 96. Non-residents' deposits | 6 |
| | 7 |
| *less* decreases in assets | |
| 99. Government securities | 7 |
| Net change | 0 |

We have now shown, using a very simple and elementary example, how the national economic activity can be summarised in a way that, in some degree, reflects the complex movements of economic resources, and the claims on these, from group to group in the economy, in the course of which the complex of prices, including the prices of debts and securities from which we derive interest rates, arises. (It is necessary to qualify our statement by the words

*Changes in assets and liabilities of sectors*
*Decreases in wealth are distinguished by a negative sign*

| | Firms[1] | Households | Government | Financial institutions | Banks | Net change |
|---|---|---|---|---|---|---|
| *Income accounts* | 6 | 4 | 1 | — | — | 11 |
| *Asset-liability accounts* | | | | | | |
| (a) *Domestic claims* | | | | | | |
| Domestic bank deposits | 5 | −6 | — | — | 1 | — |
| Debts of households | 1 | −1 | — | — | — | — |
| Government securities/national debt | 5 | −1 | 3 | — | −7 | — |
| Debenture securities of firms | −1 | — | — | 1 | — | — |
| Life assurance policies | — | 1 | — | −1 | — | — |
| Equity interests in firms | −11 | 11 | — | — | — | — |
| | −1 | 4 | 3 | — | −6 | — |
| (b) *Goods and overseas claims* | | | | | | |
| Goods | 10 | — | — | — | — | 10 |
| Non-residents' bank deposits and bills of exchange | −3 | — | — | — | 6 | 3 |
| Gold and overseas currencies | — | — | −2 | — | — | −2 |
| | 7 | — | −2 | — | 6 | 11 |
| Net change | 6 | 4 | 1 | — | — | 11 |

[1] Excluding banks and financial institutions.

'in some degree', for, as already explained, we have dealt only with net changes over time and have not attempted to portray the continuous ebb and flow of goods and claims. Moreover, the omission of all movements of goods held by consumers makes the picture less complete than it would otherwise be.)

Let us now combine the summaries of the changes in the wealth controlled by each sector, which we have extracted above (see table on p. 190).

This summary is quite illuminating. First, it shows us again that the net changes in the income accounts of each sector, which we call saving, are the result of adding together all the asset changes of that sector. Secondly, when we examine the asset changes more closely we find that although individual sectors have met changes in both domestic and overseas claims held by them, *when we take all the sectors together* changes in *domestic* claims cancel out, leaving a zero change. This is what one might expect on reflection, since *A*'s claim is *B*'s liability and to change one is to change the other. On the other hand, changes in goods and in debts due from or to *non-residents* do not cancel: these are the items that constitute changes in the real wealth of the community. The changes in goods and overseas net assets are the *gross investment* for the period, and, because the sum of all changes in assets is, by definition, equal to saving, and domestic claims cancel out, this gross investment is shown to be the same magnitude as aggregate saving. We have thus demonstrated the mechanism of the *ex post* savings-investment equality: it is an accounting truism.

This analysis also brings out the fact that the production and sale by a business of goods and services to non-residents is, from a wealth-creating viewpoint, analogous to the production of additional capital equipment and stocks: in both cases national wealth has increased.

The capital account of conventional national income accounts can now be regarded as a summary of, on the one hand (on the left-hand side), the net balances of the income accounts, which are shown on the top line of our summary; and, on the other (on the right-hand side), the balances on the accounts relating to goods and overseas net assets which together make up investment and are shown in the third section of our summary. The rest of the world account can be regarded as a convenient analysis of the overseas transactions, the sum of which represents one component of investment. Neither account is an essential part of the complete scheme we have just sketched. We include them here so that readers can see how they are related to it.

*Combined capital account*

| | | | |
|---|---|---|---|
| Saving: | | Investment: | |
| Firms | 6 | Domestic | 10 |
| Households | 4 | Overseas | 1 |
| Government | 1 | (analysed in account below) | |
| | 11 | | 11 |

*Rest of the world*

| | | | |
|---|---|---|---|
| Imports | 7 | Exports | 10 |
| Grants to overseas government | 2 | | |
| Net investment abroad | 1 | | |
| | 10 | | 10 |

By setting out these two accounts in this way the double-entry form of the conventional accounts is preserved. The data could, however, be presented in some such form as this:

| | | |
|---|---|---|
| 1. Saving, analysed by sector: | | |
| Firms | | 6 |
| Households | | 4 |
| Government | | 1 |
| Total | | 11 |
| 2. Investment, analysed by type: | | |
| Domestic: | | |
| Fixed capital formation | 8 | |
| Value of physical increases in stocks | 2 | 10 |
| Overseas: | | |
| Exports | 10 | |
| *less* Imports and grants | 9 | 1 |
| Total | | 11 |

One difficulty that is perhaps worth mentioning is connected with the problem of valuation. We have assumed in our accounts that there is no *inconsistency* of valuation: that, for example, if *A* acquires a claim on *B*, then the increase in value of *A*'s wealth recorded in the accounts exactly equals the decrease recorded for *B*. For the purpose of the accounts any inconsistency is ignored. If it were not so, the accounts might record an increase or decrease of value in a claim in one sector not offset elsewhere in that, or another, sector. It would follow that the recorded savings of that sector would be correspondingly greater or less and, since there would be no corresponding change in the opposite direction elsewhere, recorded savings in aggregate would no longer equal the recorded value of changes in physical goods plus or minus changes in overseas assets. Nevertheless, in real life such inconsistencies do, of course, occur, and we have to accept the fact that this is one of the aspects of life not susceptible of satisfactory treatment in accounts. We have in this connexion to remember that valuations are very vague affairs, whether we are concerned with claims or with goods. Indeed, value in the usual economic sense of market value can really only be said to exist at all at the moment when, and if, the thing valued is bought, sold or otherwise exchanged. Thus we have again a reminder of the abstract nature of our figures which, indeed, are really no more than *indicators* more or less vaguely related to the events they portray.

The system we have sketched above is, we emphasise, no more than an outline. Others will be able to develop or improve on our scheme. In particular there are three main ways in which any system such as this can be extended or simplified. First, the degree of compression over *time*—that is, the detail recorded in each account—may be changed: the accounts can be made to reflect less or more the continuous changes that are taking place in the economy, as distinct from the *net* effects of those changes. The net changes shown in our accounts could, in theory, be analysed more and more into their components until, at the limit, the hourly ebb and flow of assets and liabilities of all kinds was classified under appropriate heads.

Secondly, the classification by *types of transactor*—that is, the number of sectors—can be changed. The five-sector analysis we have used could, in concept at least, be extended by sub-division of sectors until at last each conceivable activity of each person in the economy would be given its own sector.

Thirdly, the classification within each sector by *types of asset and liability*—that is, the number of accounts in each sector—can be varied. On the one hand we could have, in concept at least, a classification in each sector in which a separate account was provided to record the movements of every conceivable form of asset and liability; while on the other hand we could restrict our accounts in any sector to such a simple set of goods and claims; or goods, money, and non-money claims.

3. *The United Kingdom financial accounts*

Statistics of transactions in financial assets have been compiled for the United Kingdom since 1955. They are published on a quarterly basis in *Financial Statistics* (issued monthly by the Central Statistical Office) and on an annual basis in tables in the national income Blue Book. These financial accounts, taken together with the national income accounts, present a picture of the asset structure of the United Kingdom economy closely related to the asset structure analysis we have set out above. In this section we discuss the relation between the two approaches and briefly describe the form of the United Kingdom Financial Accounts.

We start with the summary table on p. 190 which sets out the changes in assets and liabilities of our five sectors. Firstly, we distinguish between assets held as goods and assets-liabilities held in financial form and note the accounting truism implicit in the summary table that, for each sector:

surplus on income account (saving)
= net acquisition of goods plus net acquisition of financial assets.

Thus, for the firms sector, saving is 6, acquisition of goods (gross domestic investment) is 10 and net acquisition of financial assets (the sum of all other entries in the firms column of the table) is $-4$. And secondly, it can readily be seen that the summary table can be set out in such a way that the balance of payments transactions are regarded as transactions between the five sectors and an additional sector, the overseas sector. For, condensing the table further for ease of exposition, it becomes:

| | Firms | Banks | Other sectors | Net charge |
|---|---|---|---|---|
| *Income accounts* | 6 | — | 5 | 11 |
| *Asset-liability accounts* | | | | |
| Domestic claims | −1 | −6 | 7 | — |
| Goods | 10 | — | — | 10 |
| Overseas claims | −3 | 6 | −2 | 1 |
| Net change | 6 | — | 5 | 11 |

Or, alternatively, introducing an overseas sector, we have:

| | Firms | Banks | Other home sectors | Overseas | Net change |
|---|---|---|---|---|---|
| *Income accounts* | 6 | — | 5 | −1 | 10 |
| *Asset-liability accounts* | | | | | |
| Domestic claims | −1 | −6 | 7 | — | — |
| Goods | 10 | — | — | — | 10 |
| Overseas claims | −3 | 6 | −2 | −1 | — |
| Net change | 6 | — | 5 | −1 | 10 |

The transactions of the overseas sector with the home sectors are of course, the negative of the transactions of the home sectors with the overseas sector and, in particular, the surplus on income account of the overseas sector of – 1 is the negative of the country's balance of payments current surplus. As a result of adding the overseas sector, the total net change, over all sectors, of overseas claims is zero, as is the total net change of domestic claims.

In the light of the discussion so far, the summary table of changes in assets and liabilities can be re-arranged to distinguish between goods and financial assets and to exhibit the transactions of the overseas sector. (We do not reproduce all the detail of the table but the reader will have no difficulty in completing it.)

| | Firms | Banks | Other home sectors | Overseas sector | Total |
|---|---|---|---|---|---|
| *Income accounts* (=saving) | 6 | — | 5 | −1 | 10 |
| *less* Gross domestic investment | −10 | — | — | — | −10 |
| Net acquisition of financial assets | −4 | — | 5 | −1 | — |
| Of which: | | | | | |
| Domestic claims | −1 | −6 | 7 | — | — |
| Overseas claims | −3 | 6 | −2 | −1 | — |

This is very similar to the form of presentation of the official United Kingdom statistics to which we now turn.

The United Kingdom statistics set out inter-sectoral accounts for the following sectors: personal, industrial and commercial companies, banks, insurance companies and superannuation funds, other financial institutions, public sector and overseas sector. (The public comprises central and local government and public corporations.) The sectors are a little more disaggregated than in our schematic analysis of this chapter except that the public corporations are merged, not with the rest of the industrial sector, but with government.

We shall look briefly at the United Kingdom accounts in two stages: first, at the derivation of each sector's 'net acquisition of financial assets' from the national income savings and capital formation estimates, and second at the financial transactions accounts themselves. The discussion will be in terms of the actual estimates for 1965.

It is sufficient simply to consider the derivation of the change in financial assets of the personal sector. The principles of the calculation are the same for the other sectors and, moreover, the personal sector is the only one (apart from the overseas sector) common to the financial accounts and the United Kingdom national income accounts for 1965 which we have set out in Chapter 5, Table 5*a*. If the reader looks back at the capital account (account VI of Table 5*a*), he will see that personal sector saving in 1965 amounted to £2,051m. (This amount is before providing for additions to tax and any other reserves and for depreciation and stock appreciation; additions to reserves were £140m and saving after providing for addition to reserves was £1,911m.) As we explained at the end of Chapter 8, taxes on capital are not debited to the personal income and expenditure account before calculating saving. The saving figure must therefore first be adjusted by the amount of these taxes. Also, and for the same reason, there are various capital transfers (mainly capital grants from central government) which need to be taken into account. Capital transfers less taxes on capital for the personal sector amounted to −£157m in 1965. There was thus £1,894m available for investment in goods and the acquisition of financial assets.

Investment in goods falls under two heads: gross fixed capital formation and stock-building. In the United Kingdom national income accounts, the personal sector includes certain productive activities such as those of unincorporated businesses. Capital formation by these businesses together with expenditure by persons on land and dwellings is included in personal sector investment. In 1965 gross fixed capital formation by the personal sector was £1,021m. In the same year, the increase in *value* of stocks and work in progress was £146m. It should be noted that we are interested in this context in the increase in value of stocks and not in the value of physical increase in stocks for the saving figure is calculated before providing for stock appreciation.

We can now set out the sector accounts relating saving, domestic investment and changes in holdings of financial assets. As is customary, the 'saving' of the overseas sector is not entered in the first row. In our table we have aggregated, for simplicity, all the 'home' sectors other than the personal sector. Otherwise, it is similar to the official presentation except that we have added a final column showing the totals of the figures in each row.

£m

| | Personal sector | Other home sectors | Overseas sector | Un-allocated | Totals of rows |
|---|---|---|---|---|---|
| Saving[1] | 2,051 | 5,192 | | | 7,243 |
| Capital transfers *less* taxes on capital | −157 | 157 | | | — |
| *less* Gross domestic fixed capital formation | −1,021 | −5,231 | | | −6,252 |
| *less* Increase in value of stocks and work in progress | −146 | −617 | | | −763 |
| Net acquisition of financial assets | 727 | −499 | 104 | −332[2] | — |

[1] Before providing for depreciation, stock appreciation and additions to reserves.
[2] This entry equals the 'residual error' of the national income accounts reflecting the statistical discrepancy between the statistical estimates of investment and savings.

A comparison of the final column of our table with the capital account of Table 5*a* is instructive. The figure of £7,243m equals total domestic saving. The sum of the two investment figures, which amounts to £7,015m, is equal to gross domestic investment of £6,650m plus the value of stock appreciation, £365m. And the sum of all the totals in the final column equals net investment abroad less the residual error.

This completes the first stage of the discussion of the United Kingdom system and we now pass on to consider briefly the sector financial transactions account. The official account identifies some 40 different financial transaction items, each item reflecting transactions between two or more sectors. Many of the items are of course closely related to the items in our simplified scheme of section 2. To give some idea of the order of magnitude of financial transactions in an economy, a summary version of the United Kingdom account for 1965 is set out overleaf. The table groups together under the head 'Financial institutions' three separate sectors in the official account: banks, insurance companies and superannuation funds, and other financial institutions (see table p. 199).

The large value of the unidentified items is to be noted. These figures are the total result of errors in estimating savings and capital formation as well as errors and unrecorded items among the financial transactions. The large unidentified items for the personal and industrial and commercial company sectors, it is believed, largely represent transactions in stocks and shares and movements in trade credit.

## 4. *Conclusion*

A person interested in the economic life of a nation who wished to catalogue his subject matter might picture it laid out on a vast chess board, on which each piece consisted of either (*a*) a person; or (*b*) a physical resource of some kind under some particular person's control—land or equipment or goods ready for consumption or knowledge not generally available, having economic value, and so on; or (*c*) a claim, positive or negative, under the control of, or the obligation of, some person—money, shares in companies, debt, etc. In this way each separate kind of resource or claim under the control of a particular person would be given a square of its own, while the personal abilities and skills of individuals, which in a free society belong to themselves, would be represented on the board by the persons themselves. There would thus be an exhaustive catalogue of what might be called the 'fundamental atoms' of economics, each on its own labelled square. A celestial economist of superhuman intellect capable of absorbing and digesting the vast mass of detail so presented might, providing he was aware of all the potential uses to which human skill and ability and all other resources could be put, and of the desires and intentions of each person, be able not only to assess the degree of command over physical resources at present exercised by the people of this nation as compared with other

UNITED KINGDOM TRANSACTIONS IN FINANCIAL ASSETS, 1965

£m

| | Personal Sector | Industrial and Commercial Companies | Financial Institutions | Public Sector | Overseas Sector | Unallocated |
|---|---|---|---|---|---|---|
| 1. Notes, coin and bank deposits | 1,287 | 322 | −1,893 | −154 | 494 | −56 |
| 2. Government debt | 226 | −220 | 819 | −796 | −102 | 73 |
| 3. Bank lending | 39 | −553 | 872 | 3 | −361 | — |
| 4. Loans for house purchase | −689 | — | 550 | 139 | — | — |
| 5. Company and overseas securities | −685 | −4 | 651 | — | 38 | — |
| 6. Funds of life assurance | 1,173 | — | −1,173 | — | — | — |
| 7. Overseas assets | — | 193 | −3 | −138 | −52 | — |
| 8. Other identified assets | 26 | −227 | 238 | −6 | — | −31 |
| Total identified assets | 1,377 | −489 | 61 | −952 | 17 | −14 |
| Unidentified items | —650 | 686 | 30 | 165 | 87 | −318 |
| Net acquisition of financial assets | 727 | 197 | 91 | −787 | 104 | −332 |

Notes: Item 1 includes deposits with other financial institutions.
Item 2 includes local authority debt.
Item 3 includes hire purchase debt.
Item 6 includes life assurance and superannuation schemes.

nations, or with themselves at earlier times, but also, like Laplace's supreme mathematician with respect to the physical world, to predict what would happen to that nation and to each member of it in the economic sphere and the prices at which all goods, services and claims would exchange. In other words, he might be able to *assess the wealth* and *forecast the economic future* of the nation.

Our celestial economist might, as time unfolded, picture to himself a succession of such giant chess boards, on each of which at a given moment of time was displayed in the way we have described the people and their resources and claims. Comparison of one such picture with the one preceding it would show the change in the claims and goods controlled by each person; if, like a cinema film, the successive pictures were brought close together in time the beholder would begin to see a continuous rise and fall in the possessions of men: goods and claims would move from one person to another, there would be continuous human activity, goods would appear where none had before existed and others would disappear from sight.

Our aim in this chapter has been to expand the framework of conventional national income accounts into one which approximates a little more closely to such a picture. In particular, this method of presenting the figures may not only suggest ways of interpreting economic statistics after the event, but may help to provide a rough kind of framework for the semi-intuitive tracing of expected economic events and inter-relations which is involved in economic forecasting.

The celestial economist, in fact, epitomises all economists: the translation by him of his knowledge of the possibilities open to men in their manipulation of resources, of their relations with one another and of their desires and intentions into correct predictions symbolises such limited prediction as sensible economists allow themselves. The logical processes by which he reaches his forecasts symbolise the dynamic models of the theoretical economist. The statement of the problem facing him shows how humble the economist must be, for it will be noticed that not only must the forecaster know the minds of men—which for limited purposes and periods may be reflected in more or less reliable statistical laws—but if he wishes to probe more than a month or two into the future, must be able to forecast not only the course of natural phenomena, but the path of future human discovery in all the realms of knowledge.

Among the theoretical models the Keynesian type supplies, so to speak, a crutch to support the intuition in exercises of this kind: it is inadequate as a description of economic activity in the aggregate, but probably better than anything that preceded it. The more advanced mathematical models which are now being developed will, no doubt, improve the design of the crutch; but intuition will still have a big job to do, and economic forecasting will remain an art.

# GUIDE TO FURTHER READING

*Apart from the references in the text,* the reader may find it useful to consult the following works in association with each Part of the book:

### PART I

Richard and Nancy Ruggles, *National Income Accounts and Income Analysis* (2nd ed.), New York 1956.

Geer Stuvel, *Systems of Social Accounts,* Oxford 1965.

Moshe Yanovsky, *Social Accounting Systems,* London 1965.

Richard and Giovanna Stone, *National Income and Expenditure* (8th, revised, ed.), Cambridge 1966.

Wilfred Beckerman, *An Introduction to National Income Analysis,* London 1968.

All these works cover much the same ground as this book. The Ruggles' and Beckerman works are also useful for Part II. The Stuvel work offers detailed criticism of the United Kingdom national accounts. The principles and practise of compilation followed in the United Kingdom accounts are discussed in

Central Statistical Office, *National Income Statistics: Sources and Methods,* 1968.

International recommendations on systems of national accounts:

United Nations, *A system of national accounts and supporting tables,* New York 1964.

OECD, *A standardised system of national accounts,* Paris 1959.

### PART II

A more detailed exposition of the problems of measuring real product:

Richard Stone, *Quantity and Price Indexes in National Accounts*, OECD, Paris 1956.

National budgeting is explained and its application discussed in

C. Clark and G. Stuvel (Eds.), 'Income Redistribution and the Statistical Foundations of Economic Policy', *Income and Wealth*, Series X, Cambridge 1965.

It is fortunate that the founder of input-output analysis has recently brought together some of his recent contributions of an expository character in

W. W. Leontief, *Input-Output Economics*, Oxford 1966.

A useful short introduction to the subject which includes an elementary exposition of matrix algebra is

William H. Miernyk, *The Elements of Input-Output Analysis*, New York 1965.

Analyses of developments (past and prospective) in the United Kingdom economy are given in various articles of

*National Institute Economic Review* (quarterly) (National Institute of Economic and Social Research, London).

*Economic Trends* (monthly) (Central Statistical Office, HMSO, London)

*Bank of England Quarterly Bulletin.*

## PART III

General discussion of financial flows analysis and its statistical implementation is found in

National Bureau of Economic Research, 'The Flow of Funds Approach to Social Accounting', *Studies in Income and Wealth*, no. 26, Princeton 1962.

Useful texts covering both national income accounting and flow of funds analysis are

Ingvar Ohllson, *On National Accounting*, 1955.

John P. Powelson, *National Income and Flow-of-funds Analysis*, New York 1960.

In addition to the works listed above, a number of periodicals frequently contain articles on national income and social accounting. Probably the most useful are

*Journal of the Royal Statistical Society*, London

*Review of Income and Wealth*, Yale

*Staff Papers* (International Monetary Fund)

*Review of Economics and Statistics*, Harvard.

# INDEX